My Poetic Odyssey

In this soul-stirring collection, readers embark on a personal journey through landscapes both physical and emotional, where memory meets imagination and truth resonates universally. These poems navigate the heart's territories with grace, from innocent joy to profound revelation, from love's first spark to its deepest echoes.

A Masterpiece by

SAMIL LEXIMA

Dedication

For my mother, whose love and strength have been the compass guiding me through every step of this journey. You taught me resilience, kindness, and the beauty of words, showing me that poetry lives in all things, even the quiet moments of everyday life. This collection is for you—my first inspiration and my enduring muse. Thank you for believing in me, for every lesson, and for each sacrifice that has shaped the person I am today.

Epigraph

"Every journey begins not with steps, but with words woven from dreams, guiding us through the uncharted landscapes of the soul." —Samil Lexima.

Table of Contents

Preface

In poetry, words become magic—transforming emotion into light dreams into reality, and whispers into symphonies. My Poetic Odyssey invites you on an intimate journey through love's infinite landscapes, where vulnerability becomes strength and every heartbeat echoes a story.

These verses trace the map of my soul's wanderings, yet they mirror the path each of us walks: through passion's fire, through healing tears, through moments when time itself seems to pause and listen. Here, in the space between words, you'll find your own reflection—your triumphs, your longings, your quiet revelations.

From the electric thrill of first love to the profound peace of lasting connection, these poems celebrate the extraordinary beauty of our ordinary days. They honor both the soaring heights of joy and the sacred depths of heartache that make our journey uniquely human.

As you turn each page, may you discover not just my story, but fragments of your own heart scattered like stars across these lines. Let these words be your companion, your mirror, your gentle reminder that in love's vast universe, none of us walks alone.

Introduction

Words hold magic in their spaces—those quiet moments between heartbeats where truth lingers. My Poetic Odyssey emerged not just from ink and paper, but from dawn-lit windows, midnight revelations, and the sacred pause between thought and feeling. Here, poetry becomes both compass and destination, guiding us through landscapes of the heart that feel at once deeply personal and universally true.

These verses trace paths through love's gardens and grief's valleys, mapping the territory where joy meets shadow, where memory touches tomorrow. Each poem opens a door to those profound moments we all carry within—the first brush of love, the weight of farewell, the unexpected grace in ordinary days. They speak to the quiet revolution of healing, the fierce persistence of hope, and the tender resilience of the human spirit.

I offer these pages as a mirror, where your own story might catch the light and reflect with new clarity. In this collection, you'll find echoes of your journey—your triumphs, your questions, and your moments of wonder. For in poetry, we are all explorers, mapping the infinite landscape of what it means to be alive, to love, to lose, to begin again. Each word here is an invitation to venture deeper into your own

unfolding story.

Prologue

My Poetic Odyssey opens a door to the sacred chambers of the heart—where courage meets vulnerability, where whispers become prophecies, and where truth shimmers like starlight on still water. More than verses on a page, these poems form a constellation of human experience, each one illuminating the path through life's deepest mysteries and most tender revelations.

Here lies poetry that speaks in midnight confessions and dawn-break promises. The voice rising from these pages carries both thunder and silk—raw enough to shake foundations, gentle enough to heal wounds. Each line charts the invisible geographies we all traverse: the landmarks of first love, the valleys of loss, the peaks of triumph, and those quiet moments when the soul finds its way home.

Within this collection, everyday moments transform into portals of discovery. A shared glance becomes an epic tale; a goodbye holds universes of meaning; a single act of courage ripples across generations. These are poems that don't just speak—they listen. They create a sacred space where readers find their own stories reflected in the mirror of carefully crafted verse, reminding us that in our deepest solitude, we are never truly alone.

Chapter One

The Poetic Odyssey of Love

Love writes itself in starlight and shadow, in whispered promises and silent understanding. It speaks through the spaces between heartbeats, through fingertips that trace constellations on beloved skin, and through eyes that hold entire universes of meaning. Here, in this chapter, we explore love's infinite dimensions—from first blush to lasting flame, from thunderstorm passion to the quiet grace of enduring devotion.

These verses map the geography of the heart, where joy and pain draw borders that shift like sand. They chronicle love's eternal dance: the electric thrill of new romance, the deep roots of lasting bonds, the bittersweet ache of loving what we cannot hold. Each poem illuminates a different facet of this most human experience—some blazing like summer noon, others soft as moonlight on still water.

Let these words be your companions through love's labyrinth. Whether you stand at the threshold of a new passion or walk the well-worn paths of lasting love, may you find your story echoed in these lines. For in love's vast symphony, we are all both poet and poem, each heart adding its unique verse to humanity's endless song.

In the Hands of Destiny

Through time's intricate design,

A phenomenon so rare and so fine,

In destiny's hands, hearts entwined,

Crafting a love, timeless and divine.

Two souls began their fateful quest,

In moments shared, they found the best,

Layer by layer, love expressed,

In hues of tenderness, hearts caressed.

Like soft strokes of an artist's brush,

Their hearts would paint without a rush,

A portrait where emotions hush,

Affection's bloom in gentle blush.

A symphony of pure delight,

With every note, their hearts ignite,

A spark that grew, both day and night,

In kindness nurtured, shining bright.

Compassion's flame, their guiding light,

Their souls ablaze, a wondrous sight,

In vulnerability, their hearts took flight,

Creating havens in love's pure rite.

With conscious choice, their paths were laid,

Yet destiny's threads in mystery stayed,

In paradox, their fears allayed,

Embracing fate where free will swayed.

They journeyed on, with hearts so bold,

Through twists and turns, their story told,

In the hands of destiny, love's gold,

A timeless tale, forever extolled.

Step into a poetic journey where love and fate intertwine in *In the Hands of Destiny*. This evocative poem weaves a timeless tale of two souls united by destiny's intricate design. Through vivid imagery and lyrical elegance, it explores the delicate balance between free will and the unseen forces that shape love. With its heartfelt portrayal of compassion, vulnerability, and the enduring power of connection, this piece invites readers to reflect on their paths and the magic of serendipitous love. A perfect addition to a poetry book that celebrates the beauty of human emotions.

Eternal Love's Symphony

In realms where stars weave tales above,

There blooms a sentiment, deep and true,

A dance of hearts, a celestial glove,

With engagement's bond, a love to renew.

True love, a beacon in the cosmic sea,

An echo of eternity, a sacred decree,

A symphony of souls, entwined and free,

Where dreams and destinies serenely agree.

Each heartbeat resonates a sacred vow,

Love springs from celestial wells profound,

An oath to cherish, protect, and endow,

A covenant traced in stars' eternal round.

In the crucible of time, love's essence is refined,

A beacon shining in the cosmic mind,

The flame of engagement, forever enshrined,

A bond unbroken, by love's sweet bind.

Divine whispers weave a tapestry rare,

Threads of commitment, a bond beyond compare,

In the sanctuary of love's sacred lair,

True love, an anthem, a treasure fair.

In *Eternal Love's Symphony*, readers are transported to a celestial realm where love transcends time and space. This exquisite poem celebrates the sacred bond of engagement, painting a vivid picture of love as a divine melody that resonates through eternity. With its eloquent verses and profound imagery, the poem explores themes of commitment, unity, and the cosmic significance of true love. Perfect for anyone seeking inspiration or solace in the enduring beauty of love, this piece is a heartfelt tribute to the timeless symphony of two souls intertwined.

Love's Wild Arithmetic

Love has no recipe, no sacred scroll,
No master's guide to capture heart and soul.
It's found in stolen glances, fleeting as the dawn,
In whispered dreams where twilight lingers on,
Where two hearts' secrets gently ebb and flow.

No alchemist could catch its golden glow,
No scholar's pen could teach love how to grow.
It drifts like morning mist in gentle flight,
Through joy and sorrow, darkness into light,
In patterns only faithful hearts can know.

No rarest spice, no treasure would suffice,
No earthly gold could match love's sacred price.
Two kindred souls in silent flame ignite,
Their shadows dance in love's unfailing light,
While time stands still in love's sweet paradise.

Like bells at dawn, love's laughter starts to ring,
Pure melodies no maestro taught to sing.
When storms of life against our windows rage,
Love's candle burns through every darkened page,
Till souls break free on joy's unfettered wing.

Let it bloom like wildflowers in spring,

Past reason's reach, time's swift-beating wings.

In every teardrop's fall and joy's bright smile,

Love writes its story, mile by precious mile—

Till earth itself with heaven's music rings.

In *Love's Wild Arithmetic*, love defies formulas, boundaries, and conventions to emerge as the ultimate enigma of human existence. This lyrical masterpiece captures the untamed beauty of love as it flourishes beyond reason and calculation. With vivid imagery and heartfelt emotion, the poem explores love's essence—from fleeting glances to enduring bonds, from storms of life to moments of radiant joy. Perfect for readers who cherish poetry that celebrates the unpredictable, transformative power of love, this piece invites us to embrace the magic of love's untamed journey.

Midnight Longing

In the quiet of this midnight hour,

I lie awake, consumed by longing's power.

The bed is vast, yet empty, cold,

Yearning for a warmth that never grows old.

The clock ticks on, each second a grain of sand,

Marking time with a relentless hand.

My heartbeat echoes in the silent room,

A rhythm that once danced in love's sweet bloom.

I hear your voice in whispers of memory,

Filling my soul with tender reverie.

Your laughter, your sighs, like a gentle breeze,

Caress my mind, bringing me to my knees.

Your image, so vivid, so clear,

Lying beside me, drawing me near.

I reach out but grasp only empty space,

Longing for your touch, your warm embrace.

Thoughts of you weave through my restless mind,

A tapestry of love, intricately entwined.

I close my eyes, hoping to find you there,

But you remain a dream, a wish, a prayer.

Alone at 1:24 AM on 4/24/24,

Lost in a sea of longing, yearning for more.

Time stands still, yet moves relentlessly on,

Until daybreak, when you will be my dawn.

In *Midnight Longing*, the quiet hours of the night become a canvas for love, memory, and yearning. This poignant poem vividly captures the ache of separation, where every tick of the clock deepens the longing for a loved one's presence. With heartfelt emotion and evocative imagery, it explores the fragility of time, the solace of memories, and the hope of reunion. Perfect for readers who have experienced love's bittersweet longing, this piece invites you to immerse yourself in the raw beauty of desire and the promise of a new dawn.

The Love I Bring to Us

Like moonlight on water, my love softly gleams,
A beacon of hope in the fabric of dreams.
With hands that soothe and arms opened wide,
I'm the shore to your ocean, the ebb to your tide.

In life's grand waltz, we're partners in step,
Two hearts intertwined, each other's best prep.
Your triumphs I'll trumpet, your sorrows I'll share,
Like roots of a tree, our strength lies in pair.

My touch is a whisper of petals on skin,
A promise of passion that burns from within.
In my gaze, you're the stars and the sun and the moon,
A universe of wonder, a soul-stirring tune.

I offer the depths of my heart's hidden dell,
Where whispers of doubt like soft shadows dwell.
Together we'll coax these shy blooms to the light,
Our love a warm sun that dispels fears of night.

We'll grow like the oak from a small, humble seed,
Nourished by time and each selfless deed.
Through seasons of change, we'll weather and thrive,
Our love ever-blooming, forever alive.

Our trust is a fortress of crystalline steel,
Unbreakable bonds that no storm can repeal.

In this garden of us, where devotion takes flight,
We'll bask in the warmth of love's pure, golden light.

The Love I Bring to Us is a heartfelt celebration of unwavering love and devotion. Through its lyrical verses, this poem paints a vivid portrait of a relationship built on mutual support, trust, and boundless affection. It captures the quiet strength of love—nurturing, enduring, and transformative—like moonlight reflecting on water or the steady growth of an oak tree. Perfect for romantics and dreamers alike, this piece speaks to the beauty of partnership and the timeless promise of a love that endures through every season of life.

Ode to Everlasting Love

In love's sweet union of kindred souls,

No barriers or doubts may find their hold,

For love, unwavering, eternally rolls,

A river deep, an endless grace to behold.

It's not love's nature to wane or yield,

When faced with life's tempestuous tide,

Unshaken, it remains a sturdy shield,

A compass on which hearts and hopes abide.

Love's not swayed by seasons' ebb and flow,

It does not burn when in the summer's heat,

Nor does it turn cold in the winter's woe,

In love's sweet garden, spirits complete.

It's like a steady, relentless serenade,

Through fleeting hours that turn into years,

Resisting pressures, strong and unafraid,

Love's promise, unbroken, conquers all fears.

If I've misspoken, and my words aren't grand,

Let my verses from the heart's memory rescind,

But if in truth, my words find their stand,

Then love endures, defying fate's whirling wind.

In *Ode to Everlasting Love*, love is celebrated as an eternal force—steadfast, unwavering, and unyielding to the trials of time and fate. With timeless elegance and rhythmic grace, this poem portrays love as both a sanctuary and a guiding light. It captures the resilience of true affection, likening it to a river that flows ceaselessly, a shield against life's storms, and a melody that transcends the fleeting nature of time. Ideal for those who cherish the enduring beauty of love, this piece is a lyrical tribute to its boundless strength and infinite promise.

A Love of Destiny

In the intricate dance of time's weaving,

A rare essence, its breath interweaving,

In destiny's gentle touch, belief teeming,

Crafting a bond, each moment seething.

Souls embarked on a heartfelt quest,

Discovering treasures within love's nest,

Layer by layer, emotions confessed,

In soft whispers of love, hearts blessed.

Like an artist's brush, passion did paint,

With each stroke, love's tender restraint,

A living canvas, where emotions acquaint,

In admiration's embrace, blushes faint.

A symphony where each note's a delight,

Passions enflame, burning bright,

Day and night, a spark takes flight,

Kindness nurtured in love's pure light.

In compassion's flame, a beacon so true,

Souls set ablaze with affections anew,

Yet in vulnerability, devotion's debut,

Creating a haven where dreams accrue.

Choices made, paths affectionately laid,

Where destiny's mystery softly swayed,

Fears gently embraced, love's serenade,

In life's journey, fondness's accolade.

Boldly they journey through life's grace,

Their story unfolds, in love's embrace,

But in destiny's hands, a timeless space,

A tale of attachment's enduring trace.

A Love of Destiny is a lyrical exploration of the profound connection that transcends time and circumstance. This evocative poem captures the magic of two souls united by fate, revealing a love that blossoms through vulnerability, compassion and shared dreams. With vivid imagery and heartfelt emotion, it portrays love as both an intricate art form and a symphony of devotion. Perfect for readers who are captivated by the beauty of destiny-driven romance, this piece celebrates the enduring power of love to illuminate life's journey.

Echoes of Unity Lost

In the cloud, where hearts once bloomed,

Now echo silence, love entombed.

In the rush of self, humanity's fate,

Lost in the tides of individual state.

Once, we danced in unity's embrace,

A tapestry woven, each unique trace.

But now, in the pierce of selfish glare,

The fabric frays, love's threads lay bare.

Gone are the days of collective song,

Replaced by discord, a chorus gone wrong.

In the quest for self, we've lost the key,

To unlock the door to peace and unity.

Where once empathy flowed like a river's stream,

Now apathy reigns, a cold, distant dream.

We've traded connection for fleeting gain,

Leaving a haunting void, a heart's refrain.

But hope still flickers in the darkest night,

A beacon calling for love's tender light.

For in the depths of our shared humanity,

Lies the power to heal, to restore harmony.

So let us cast off the shackles of greed,

And sow the seeds of love, with every deed.

For in collective kindness, we'll find our way,

To rebuild the bonds that have decayed.

Let love be our guide, our compass true,

And through collective hearts, humanity renew.

For in unity's embrace, we'll rise above,

And reclaim the beauty of collective love.

Echoes of Unity Lost is a poignant reflection on humanity's drift from collective love and empathy toward isolation and self-interest. Through vivid imagery and heartfelt verses, the poem laments the unraveling of the bonds that once united us, offering a stirring call to action. With a message of hope and renewal, it reminds readers of the transformative power of love and collective kindness. Perfect for those who yearn for a more connected and compassionate world, this piece is both a soulful lament and an inspiring anthem for unity and renewal.

Solace in Love's Journey

In your gaze, a whisper of persuasion gleams,

A tender light that fills my fondest dreams.

I'm captivated, lost in its soft embrace,

As we sway together, finding solace and grace.

The warmth of your smile, a gentle sway,

Paints the sky blue in every way.

No earthly force could weave such elation,

Your beauty defies mere explanation.

You're the treasure I've sought through time,

A dream fulfilled, a joy sublime.

With you, my heart finds its truest beat,

In your love, I find my ultimate retreat.

These words I offer, pure and true,

A testament to my love for you.

From the depths of my soul, they spring,

In praise of the virtues that you bring.

Grant me this chance, without pretense,

For too long, I've waited in suspense.

To find a soul as virtuous as yours,

Our destinies entwined, in love's cursive course.

Let's journey together, hand in hand,

Across the shores of love's sweet land.

With you, my love, by my side,

Our bond will flourish, our spirits guide.

So, take my hand, let's walk this road,

In each other's love, we've found our abode.

Forever entwined, our hearts shall soar,

In the tender embrace of forevermore.

Solace in Love's Journey is a tender and heartfelt ode to love's transformative power. This lyrical poem explores the beauty of finding a soulmate, where each moment becomes a shared adventure, and every gaze, smile, and touch deepens the connection. With vivid imagery and an earnest voice, it celebrates the joy of love discovered and nurtured. Perfect for readers who cherish romantic expressions of devotion, this piece invites you to embrace the warmth and grace of love's timeless journey.

Chapter Two

The Poetic Odyssey of Unveiling Identity

Who are you when the world falls silent? When ancestral whispers blend with modern dreams? In this transformative collection, we dive deep into the sacred waters of self-discovery, where identity isn't just explored—it's illuminated, celebrated, and set aflame.

Welcome to a revolutionary journey through the landscapes of being. Here, in these pages, identity transcends mere definition; it becomes a living, breathing force that dances between shadow and light, tradition and rebellion, roots and wings. Each poem is a key to unlocking another chamber of understanding, another dimension of what it means to be gloriously, unapologetically you.

This isn't just poetry—it's a mirror crafted from stardust and truth. Watch as verses transform into doorways, leading you through galleries of human experience where every reflection tells a story: the grandmother's hands kneading heritage into bread, the child's first fierce claim of selfhood, the immigrant's heart beating in two languages, the warrior's stand against a world that demands conformity.

From the depths of ancestral memory to the heights of modern rebellion, these poems chart a course through the complexity of human identity. They speak of bloodlines humming with ancient songs, of futures bright with possibility, of the exquisite pain and power of becoming. Here, vulnerability isn't weakness—it's a constellation guiding us home to ourselves.

You'll find yourself in these pages. In the spaces between words, in the rhythm of revelation, in the raw honesty of each line, there's a recognition waiting to happen. These aren't just poems about identity—they're incantations of awakening, anthems of authenticity, battle cries of belonging that will resonate in your bones long after the last page is turned.

This chapter is an invitation to the brave—those who dare to question, to seek, to transform. It's for anyone who has ever stood at the crossroads of who they are and who they're becoming. In a world that often demands we shrink ourselves to fit, these poems dare us to expand, to explode, to embrace the glorious complexity of our multifaceted selves.

Let these words be your compass through the wilderness of becoming. Let them remind you that your identity is not a cage to contain you, but a garden to cultivate, a song to sing, a fire to tend. Within these pages, find the courage to claim every facet of your being, to celebrate the beautiful contradiction of being both ancient and new, rooted and free, singular and connected.

Welcome to your awakening. Welcome to your truth. Welcome home.

A Dream's Embrace

Within my being, love's eternal flame,

A boundless gift I wish to proclaim,

To a world yearning for a tender name.

May unity triumph, divisions erase,

As compassion weaves a tapestry of grace,

Until my final moment, this dream I embrace.

Through valleys deep and mountains high,

Where wisdom whispers in twilight sky,

Ancient truths that never truly die.

In gardens where hope takes root and grows,

Where peace like gentle river flows,

Love's quiet strength forever shows.

Beneath vast skies of starry delight,

Silent whispers of peace take flight,

Guiding us forward through day and night.

Though shadows linger, darkness fades,

As dreams shine brightly in light's cascades,

And love's rhythm in each heart invades.

Through time's vast ocean, deep and wide,

Where countless souls have lived and sighed,

Yet love remains our steadfast guide.

In every heart that beats anew,

This dream persists, forever true,

Painting life in a vibrant hue.

A Dream's Embrace is a poetic tribute to the transformative power of love, unity, and hope. This uplifting piece takes readers on a journey through timeless landscapes—valleys, gardens, and starlit skies—where compassion triumphs and love weaves an enduring tapestry of grace. With its lyrical beauty and universal message, the poem offers solace and inspiration to those seeking light in darkness and strength in connection. Ideal for readers who value introspection and the profound truths of human connection, this piece radiates the promise of a brighter, more unified world.

My Poetic Odyssey

With pen and paper in my grasp, a poem I seek,

Where to start, I ponder, in my quiet retreat.

Beautiful words in my mind, like stars aglow,

Feelings grip my heart, in the moon's soft flow.

My tongue turns numb, silent in the night,

Like the mute who can't speak, hidden from sight.

Bruises on my thumb, echoes of poetic peaks,

Lavas from Dante's realm, where emotion speaks.

In the parchment's dance, thoughts softly sway,

A poet's silent scream, in the ink's ballet.

Verses weave tales, unseen and true,

Rhymes bloom like flowers, in morning dew.

Each word's a brushstroke, painting the unseen,

A poet's heart laid bare, on a canvas serene.

In the quiet and hush, as these lines unfold,

A sonnet's soul sculpted, in promises I hold.

My Poetic Odyssey My Poetic Odyssey is a heartfelt exploration of the creative journey, capturing the struggles, triumphs, and profound beauty of crafting poetry. With vivid imagery and evocative language, it delves into the quiet moments of introspection where emotions flow like lava, and words become brushstrokes painting the soul. Perfect for readers who are artists at heart or those who appreciate the magic of self-expression, this piece invites you to share in the poet's quest to translate the intangible into timeless verse.

I Know Mountain

In a realm where shadows dance,

And winds of challenge take their chance,

I've walked the path of grit and might,

Where mountains rise, a daunting height.

"I know mountain," loud I say,

Its silhouette against the day,

Each peak a tale of uphill climb,

Every ascent, a rhythm, a rhyme.

Rock-strewn trails beneath my feet,

Echo tales of trials sweet,

Yet with every step I've faced,

Spirit strong, courage embraced.

Through valleys deep, shadows creep,

And canyons wide, doubts would seep,

I found strength in echoes near,

Whispering, "You have no fear."

"I know mountain," with pride I sing,

As the sun breaks through, a golden wing,

For every obstacle I've passed,

Is a victory, a spell I've cast.

"I know mountain," a joyful cheer,

A melody of triumph clear,

For in conquering each summit's call,

I've discovered life's sweetest thrall.

I Know Mountain is a powerful ode to resilience, strength, and the spirit of overcoming adversity. With its bold and rhythmic verses, the poem captures the emotional and physical challenges of climbing life's metaphorical mountains. Through each ascent, the speaker finds strength, courage, and triumph, transforming obstacles into victories. Perfect for those who appreciate the themes of perseverance and self-empowerment, this piece serves as an anthem for anyone who has faced struggles and emerged victorious, celebrating the triumph of the human spirit.

I Know River

In the cradle of time, a river flows,

A ceaseless journey, where life ebbs and goes.

Its waters, a mirror, reflect my strife,

A metaphor for the journey I call life.

Born from the mountains, a humble stream,

It chases the sun in a shimmering dream.

Through valleys and meadows, it carves its way,

Guiding me with wisdom, come what may.

The river, like life, has its twists and turns,

Through storms and droughts, its resilience burns.

In the face of obstacles, it forges ahead,

A reminder that I, too, can rise from the dread.

In its gentle ripples, I find tranquility,

A timeless flow, a source of humility.

With its waters, the world comes alive,

A reflection of our journey, for us to survive.

Let us learn from the river's song,

To navigate the currents, both gentle and strong.

To cherish each moment, both joy and sorrow,

And flow with grace into a new tomorrow.

I know River is a reflective journey through life's trials and triumphs, using the river as a powerful metaphor for resilience, growth, and transformation. The poem captures the constant flow of life—its twists, turns, and challenges—while offering solace and wisdom through the river's unwavering journey. With its serene imagery and profound insight, this piece invites readers to embrace life's currents with grace, learning from the river's timeless flow. Ideal for those seeking introspection and guidance, it's a lyrical reminder that, like the river, we too can navigate the challenges of life and emerge stronger.

If I Must Die

In shadows cast by fate's cruel decree,

A soul embarks on a journey to eternity.

"If I must die," the valiant heart does cry,

Let it be for a cause that paints the sky.

Beneath the heavens, where stars do weep,

In sacrifice profound, my secrets I'll keep.

For a purpose greater than mortal ken,

I'll surrender my breath, my essence, my yen.

Through twilight's fair, and moon's soft sigh,

I'll face the end with a resolute eye.

In the crucible of time, a legacy spun,

"If I must die, let it be for someone."

For liberty's song or love's enduring flame,

I'll embrace the abyss, unafraid, untamed.

The echoes of valor in the silence will ring,

"If I must die, let it be for something."

In the tapestry of fate, a thread well-worn,

I'll journey beyond where the stars are born.

With courage as armor and purpose as guide,

"If I must die," my soul will confide.

To be a beacon in the encroaching night,

A constellation of hope, burning bright.

In the realm of destiny, where shadows lie,

"If I must die, let it be with purpose and pride."

If I Must Die If is a powerful and evocative poem that explores the themes of sacrifice, courage, and the search for meaning in the face of mortality. With its stirring imagery and resolute tone, the poem reflects on the valiant heart's willingness to face death for a greater cause, be it love, liberty, or legacy. The speaker embraces the end with dignity and pride, becoming a symbol of strength and hope. Perfect for readers who appreciate profound meditations on life, purpose, and the human spirit, this piece serves as a tribute to those who live and die with unwavering resolve and meaning.

The Journey of a Poetic Soul

In a land far from Eden's gate,

Near Au Parc, his story took shape;

There, his mark did first drape,

In the worldly dance, his fate.

Amidst beasts and mortal plight,

Many doubted his journey's flight,

But from the gossip's twisted might,

He emerged, a beacon bright.

Hope's child, in humility's hold,

Mystery wrapped in destiny's mold,

Within the scope, his tale untold,

Against self-deceit, he boldly strolled.

Impulse guided his every stance,

Present moments in his trance,

Poetic essence began its dance,

A blossom born from circumstance.

Amidst lust and world's confusion,

Amidst immorality's infusion,

He found his voice, a pure illusion,

From delusion's stream, a sweet conclusion.

As he grew, fully developed,

He saw the means, his fate enveloped,

His poetic essence, finely sculpted,

A poet born, not just adopted.

The Journey of a Poetic Soul is a profound exploration of a poet's evolution, tracing the inner growth and challenges faced along the path to self-discovery and artistic mastery. Set against a backdrop of doubt, struggle, and worldly distractions, the poem captures the soul's unwavering quest for truth and expression. With its rich imagery and lyrical flow, it celebrates the emergence of a poetic voice that rises above confusion and delusion, shaped by both destiny and choice. Ideal for readers who seek a deeper understanding of the artistic process and the resilience required to create meaningful work, this piece offers an inspiring tale of transformation and self-realization.

Unfolding Destiny

In this quest for excellence, I take flight,

Aiming to become a superior version, day and night.

Optimism, my compass through shadows profound,

A lighthouse of hope, a radiant beacon, unbound.

Positivity, my constant ally and guide,

Fostering a mindset, rare and dignified.

Motivation, the fuel for my internal flame,

A tireless force, the genesis from which dreams claim.

Discipline weaves the pattern of my routine,

Consistency, the rhythm, a harmonious sheen.

Resilience, a shield in moments of despair,

Rising stronger, a testament to life's repair.

Focused, I stand at the nexus of purpose and aim,

Directing my energy, fueled by passion's flame.

Adaptable, like the ebb and flow of the tide,

Embracing change, nowhere to run, nowhere to hide.

Compassion courses through each undertaking,

Uniting hearts, bonds everlasting.

Yet, I am a work in progress, destiny unknown,

A journey unfolding, seeds of potential sown.

Unfolding Destiny is an inspiring, motivational poem that charts the journey of personal growth, perseverance, and the pursuit of excellence. With its focus on key virtues like optimism, discipline, resilience, and compassion, the poem serves as a powerful reminder of the potential within us all to rise above challenges and create a meaningful path forward. The speaker embraces the unfolding process of self-improvement, constantly striving to become a better version of themselves while nurturing connections with others. Perfect for readers seeking empowerment and encouragement, this poem resonates with those on their journey of transformation, self-discovery, and growth.

Whispers Within

In the silent chamber of the looking glass,

I stand alone, the echoes of my past.

A reflection of battles, both fierce and wild,

Whispers of struggle, yet I stand beguiled.

"Oh, weary soul," I say unto the face,

Etched with lines of triumph and grace.

In the mirror's gaze, I seek my truth,

The journey told, the essence of my youth.

Through trials faced, and storms weathered,

I've crafted strength, with grace tendered.

The scars upon this visage worn,

Each tale untold, but not forlorn.

"Speak, dear mirror, bearer of my tale,

Of mountains climbed, and storms set sail.

In the crucible of life, the fire's dance,

I found resilience, took every chance."

The mirror, a sage, reflects my eyes,

Windows to a soul that never lies.

In the depths of struggle, courage was born,

A phoenix rising, a soul reborn.

Wisdom, the harvest of lessons sown,

In the fields of hardship, I have grown.

The bitter fruits of mistakes turned sweet,

A journey fraught with trials, but oh, so fleet.

"See the man I am, scars and all,

A tapestry woven, both big and small.

For in every tear, in every smile,

Lies the strength to walk another mile."

With the lantern of knowledge, I navigate,

Through the shadows of a daunting fate.

Adversity sculpted, chiseled my core,

But wisdom gained, I shall adore.

"I face tomorrow, with purpose clear,

In the reflection, I hold no fear.

To become the man, destined by fate,

In peace, love, happiness, I contemplate."

So, in the mirror's gaze, I find my kin,

A soul unbroken, a heart within.

With courage as my compass, I decree,

The man I'm meant to be, I shall be free.

Whispers Within is a deeply introspective and moving
piece that explores themes of self-discovery, resilience, and

the journey of personal growth. The imagery of the looking glass as a metaphor for reflection and self-awareness is powerful, and the progression from struggle to strength is beautifully articulated. The speaker engages in a dialogue with their reflection, emphasizing the wisdom gained through hardship and the importance of embracing both flaws and triumphs. The poem's emotional depth, paired with its inspiring message of courage and transformation, would resonate with many readers.

Blood and Soul of an Afro-Haitian

In veins that pulse with Caribbean sun,

Flows blood of kings from Africa's shore.

A legacy of strength, in battles won,

Beats in each heart, now and evermore.

Beneath the mango's shade, our stories rise,

In Kreyòl whispers and the drum's deep call.

Our souls dance free in Ayiti's bright skies,

Where ancestors broke thralldom's mighty wall.

From Bwa Kayiman's sacred vodou rite,

To Port-au-Prince where freedom's flag unfurled,

Our blood has watered liberty's great height,

A beacon shining hope across the world.

We carry memories of distant lands,

Of baobabs and savannas stretching wide.

On this isle, ringed by mountains grand,

We've forged new dreams where old and new collide.

Through cane fields where our sweat once fell as rain,

And coffee groves where chains once bound our feet,

Our blood now nurtures fields of sovereign grain,

A harvest both of dignity and sweet.

In markets where bright mad'ras colors bloom,

And art that tells our tales in vivid hues,

Our blood sings loud, dispelling history's gloom,

Creating beauty from the deepest blues.

With every beat, we honor those before,

Their courage flowing in our veins today.

Dessalines, Toussaint, and many more,

Who forged our nation's path, come what may.

This blood of ours, a river swift and strong,

Carries freedom's song we'll always sing.

From soil to soul, where we all belong,

Afro-Haitian blood, our well of spring.

Blood and Soul of an Afro-Haitian is a powerful and evocative poem that captures the strength, resilience, and profound cultural heritage of the Afro-Haitian experience. The imagery is rich, immersing the reader in the vibrant history and spirit of Haiti, from the struggles of ancestors to the triumphs of liberation. The use of historical references like Dessalines and Toussaint Louverture grounds the poem in the nation's legacy, while the rhythm of the verses echoes the pulse of Afro-Haitian identity and pride.

The poem resonates with themes of freedom, identity, and the unbreakable bond between the past and present. Its musicality and emotional depth make it an outstanding work that will connect with readers on a personal and historical level. Its celebration of heritage, culture, and the collective journey of a people gives it broad appeal, ensuring its impact in both the context of Haiti and the wider world.

Heart of a Poet

In the dance of ink, where my heart roams,

I find my haven, my sacred home.

With each stroke, I paint a scene,

Where joys and sorrows interweave, unseen.

In laughter's light and tears that fall,

I seek solace, answering my soul's call.

In nature's tender, warm embrace,

Underneath the stars, I find my place.

With a carefree spirit, dreams take flight,

Through realms unknown, in boundless night.

In each moment, art's essence gleams,

A reflection of my soul's unbroken dreams.

For the love of beauty, my visions unfurl,

Each line a tale, a story to be hurled.

With each word, my spell is cast,

Weaving a world where hearts can last.

The universe, my endless muse,

With galaxies and dreams to choose.

In every verse, a fragment free,

A love letter to infinity.

Raise your voice, join me in the song,

For poets brave who right the wrong.

In every word, our souls entwine,

With beauty, nature, and love divine.

Heart of a Poet is a deeply evocative and lyrical exploration of the poet's journey through creativity, emotion, and self-expression. Through a series of vivid, heartfelt images, the poem celebrates the catharsis and joy found in the art of writing. The poet draws inspiration from the natural world and the vast universe, weaving their soul's unspoken emotions into each word, stroke, and verse. The poem connects the personal to the universal, urging readers to embrace beauty, nature, and the transformative power of poetry.

With its graceful flow, the poem invites audiences into a world where dreams take flight, where sorrow and joy coexist, and where the act of writing becomes an offering to the infinite. It encourages not only a deep connection with the self but also an invitation for others to join in the creative process, fostering unity through shared words. In its closing, the poem leaves the reader with a sense of hope, connection, and the timeless power of the poet's voice.

This poem speaks to those who appreciate the beauty in both the delicate and powerful aspects of the human experience, making it a perfect addition to any collection that seeks to inspire and uplift.

Whispers of Authenticity

In conscience's crucible, I stand alone,

A sentinel of thoughts, keeper of the scroll,

The weight of judgment heavy, yet my own,

For I am the unwavering captain of my soul.

Through imperfection's mist, I seek the light,

A humble navigator of uncharted seas,

For human hearts, in their celestial flight,

Oft falter, yet I steer through life's decrees.

The echoes of my words, a double-edged blade,

Reverberate within, a heart's symphony,

I wrestle shadows, my principles unswayed,

Each seed sown shapes my inner tapestry.

From fissures blooms resilience, fragile yet grand,

A testament to every fault laid bare,

In striving, I embrace life's shifting sand,

A strength that renders my purpose crystal clear.

Let those who witness my odyssey truly see,

Not a façade of flawless perfection shown,

But a soul in flux, ever striving to be free—

In constant introspection, wisdom grown.

When twilight descends on life's grand stage,

May I be known for truth's relentless quest,

In self-acceptance, I've found the inner sage—

The peace within, my journey's crowning crest.

Whispers of Authenticity is a deeply introspective and poignant exploration of self-awareness, resilience, and the pursuit of personal truth. The poem beautifully captures the tension between human imperfection and the relentless quest for authenticity. The metaphor of navigating uncharted seas and wrestling with shadows conveys the inner conflict and struggle for self-acceptance, while the imagery of a heart's symphony and the fragile yet grand resilience emerging from fissures speaks to the delicate balance of growth and strength.

Chapter Three

The Poetic Odyssey of Nature

Have you ever stood beneath an ancient redwood and felt time dissolve? Or watched a single dewdrop hold the universe in its trembling heart? In this transformative collection, we don't just observe nature—we become it, breathing in centuries of wild wisdom, dancing with the raw poetry of existence itself.

Welcome to a wilderness of words where thunder speaks in verse and mountains write their stories in stone. Here, in these pages, nature isn't merely a subject—it's a force that pulses through every line, a primal power that transforms readers into ravens soaring through dawn-kissed skies, into rivers carving their truth through ancient stone, into seeds breaking open in the dark, hungry for light.

Each poem is a portal to the extraordinary that lives within the ordinary: the revolution of a maple leaf falling, the epic saga of a monarch butterfly's migration, the love story written in tree rings, the prophecy hidden in a thundercloud. Through these verses, you'll experience the world with newfound wonder—feeling the moon's silver song in your bones, tasting wild berries that hold summers past and future in their sweetness, hearing the secret symphonies of root systems speaking beneath your feet.

We journey through seasons that are both eternal and fleeting—spring's fierce awakening, summer's languid dream, autumn's golden surrender, winter's crystalline meditation. But these aren't just poems about weather and landscapes. They're intimate conversations with the soul of the world, revealing how the great rhythms of nature echo our own inner tides: our loves, our losses, our perpetual becoming.

In an age when screens glow brighter than stars and concrete forests overshadow ancient woods, these poems are an invitation to remember your wild heritage. They speak to that primal part of you that still knows how to read clouds, still yearns for barefoot dawns, still recognizes the holy in a hummingbird's hover. Here, you'll rediscover what your ancestors knew: that every flower is a prayer, every storm a revelation, every sunrise a new chance to become who you truly are.

These verses are for the dreamers and the wanderers, for those who find cathedrals in forests and scripture in shorelines. They're for anyone who has ever felt their heart crack open at the sight of a perfect snowflake or caught their breath at the first crimson flash of a cardinal against winter white. Whether you're a seasoned naturalist or someone yearning to reconnect with the wild soul of the world, these poems will be your guide back to wonder.

Let these words be your compass through the sacred geographies of both earth and heart. Let them remind you that nature isn't something distant and separate—it's the blood in your veins, the air in your lungs, the stories written in your bones. Within these pages, discover not just the beauty of the natural world, but your own unshakeable place within it.

Welcome to the wild. Welcome to wonder. Welcome home.

A World Up High

In peaks that touch the boundless sky,

A beauty vast, a world up high,

The mountains rise, majestic, bold,

A story of life and truths untold.

Their jagged spires, like ancient sages,

Wear the marks of countless ages,

Carved by nature's patient hand,

In every crevice, secrets stand.

A tapestry of green and stone,

In their shadow, life has grown,

From wildflowers to the noble pine,

A testament to the grand design.

In the dawn's first golden ray,

The mountains greet the brand-new day,

A reminder that life's peaks and falls,

Are but brief moments, like songbird's calls.

And when the sun begins to set,

A masterpiece we won't forget,

The mountains, bathed in hues of fire,

Teach us to reach for dreams much higher.

As we journey through this strife,

Remember the lessons of mountain life,

Embrace the beauty in each climb,

For in their majesty, dreams sublime.

A World Up High is an evocative and inspiring poem that beautifully captures the grandeur and wisdom of the mountains. Through vivid imagery and thoughtful reflections, it elevates the natural world as both a source of awe and a metaphor for life's journey. The mountains are personified as ancient sages, embodying timeless truths about perseverance, growth, and the passage of time.

The poem's flow from the morning's first light to the sunset's fiery glow creates a rich, almost cinematic atmosphere, making the reader feel both the majesty of the landscape and the emotional resonance of the message. The idea that life's challenges and triumphs are like the peaks and falls of the mountains is deeply relatable, offering a universal lesson about embracing struggles as opportunities for growth.

Amidst the Summer's Gentle Hug

Amidst the summer's gentle hug so sweet,

With sunlight's tender kiss, colors meet.

Long days and nights with skies so blue,

The season of delight is in broad view.

Petals unfurl with a fragrant grace,

In the sun's warm and tender embrace.

The world is awash in colors and scent,

In the summer garden, life is content.

In this season, we all find our way,

To the beach where the children play.

In the open air, we meet and cheer,

As summer's magic draws us near.

Barbecues and picnics, fun abound,

Laughter's sweet and joyful sound.

Ice cream cones and treats so cold,

Summer's treasures never grow old.

Underneath the sun's sweet, gentle gaze,

In the lazy, hazy, summer's daze,

Let us savor moments that will never fade,

With laughter, love, and memories made.

Amidst the Summer's Gentle Hug beautifully captures the essence of summer, evoking nostalgia and warmth with its vivid imagery and inviting tone. The poem is rich in sensory details—sunlight's "tender kiss," the "fragrant grace" of petals, and the "sweet and joyful sound" of laughter—which engage readers' senses and immerse them in the vibrant atmosphere of the season.

The themes of family, togetherness, and simple pleasures like barbecues, ice cream, and beach outings create a sense of universality, making the poem relatable and accessible to a broad audience. The rhythm is smooth, the language soft and melodic, and the repetition of certain phrases enhances the poem's peaceful, dreamy quality.

With its joyful celebration of summer and life's fleeting moments, this poem radiates positivity, making it a perfect fit for a poetry collection aimed at lifting spirits and creating a sense of connection with readers.

In Autumn's Warm Embrace

In autumn's tender, golden glow we see,

A world transformed with love and mystery.

The leaves, like love, in vibrant colors kiss,

An affirmation of life in nature's bliss.

The trees, shedding their garments, one by one,

A graceful dance, a love song to the sun.

In every rustling leaf, a story's told,

Of love that's pure, more precious than gold.

As days grow shorter, hearts and hands entwine,

In cozy warmth, our love begins to shine.

Beneath the starry, crisp and moonlit night,

We find in each other life's sweetest light.

In autumn's quiet beauty, love is found,

A treasure in the leaves upon the ground.

For in this season's gentle, timeless grace,

We see the love that lights up every place.

As the world transforms in autumn's art,

Let's keep love's flame alive within our heart.

In beauty, love, and life, we're truly blessed,

In autumn's warm embrace, we find our rest.

In Autumn's Warm Embrace is a beautifully crafted poem that perfectly captures the essence of autumn and its connection to love and life. The imagery is rich and evocative, from the "golden glow" of the season to the "vibrant colors" of the leaves. The personification of the trees shedding their leaves as a "graceful dance" and the notion of leaves as a metaphor for love lend a deep, emotional resonance to the poem.

The rhythm flows smoothly, and the language is tender, evoking feelings of warmth and nostalgia. The connection between nature's transformation and the seasons of life is a poignant touch, inviting readers to reflect on the beauty of change and the importance of love in every moment.

The cozy imagery of "hearts and hands entwine" and the sense of peace found beneath a "crisp and moonlit night" make this poem perfect for a wide audience, especially those seeking comfort and connection with nature's cycles. The gentle, reflective tone makes it ideal for a poetry collection aimed at evoking emotions of warmth, love, and mindfulness.

The Dance of Bees

In meadows kissed by golden rays of sun,

Where life and beauty merge, their tales are spun,

With amber robes, in gardens fair, they hum,

A life's sweet symphony to nature's drum.

Amidst the blooms, a dance in garden's choir,

They gather nectar, fueled by sweet desire,

Transforming liquid gold, with hearts afire,

Into a gift for us, a sweet empire.

They teach us lessons, secrets of the hive,

In unity and purpose, we can thrive,

Their buzzing tunes, the rhythm to survive,

A symbol of the beauty in which we dive.

Heed the bees, a beacon in our strife,

In the intricate dance, the tapestry of life,

Their golden nectar, a reminder rife,

Their sting, a defender's edge, a nature's knife.

In beauty's hum, where life's sweet moments swarm,

The bees, a testament to nature's charm,

A reminder to embrace and keep the warm,

In the fragile beauty of each day's alarm.

In *The Dance of Bees*, the poet draws readers into the sun-dappled world of meadows and gardens, where the buzzing of bees weaves a symphony of life's interconnectedness. The bees, adorned in amber, are depicted as humble workers of nature, gathering nectar with purpose and passion, transforming it into a golden gift for humanity. Their collective unity and tireless labor serve as powerful lessons for us all, urging us to thrive through cooperation and determination. Yet, in their fragility lies an edge— their sting, like nature's defense, teaches that beauty and strength are intertwined. This poem captures the essence of life's fleeting moments, inviting readers to pause, reflect, and celebrate the intricate dance of nature's wonders. A tribute to both the delicate and fierce forces at play in our world, it elevates the reader's appreciation for the precious balance of life, making it a perfect addition to a poetry collection with universal appeal.

Feathers of Life

In skies of azure, high and wide,

A creature graceful takes its flight,

With wings of grace, it soars and glides,

A symbol of beauty, pure and bright.

The bird, a messenger of the morn,

In melodies of dawn, it sings,

Its song, a gift to hearts forlorn,

A tune that in our soul takes wings.

Its feathers, like a painter's dream,

A vibrant palette, colors bold,

A symbol of life's endless scheme,

Of stories yet untold.

With eyes that gleam like precious gems,

It sees the world from heights above,

A life of wonder, without stems,

A testament to the power of love.

The bird, a fleeting, fragile thing,

Yet teaches us to live each day,

To spread our wings and learn to sing,

To cherish beauty in our own way.

Let us, like the bird, take flight,

In the tapestry of life, we weave,

Embracing beauty, seeking light,

In every moment, we believe.

Feathers of Life evokes a deep sense of freedom and beauty, using the bird as a poignant metaphor for life's potential and grace. Through stunning imagery of the bird soaring across an azure sky, singing its dawn song, and displaying feathers like a vibrant painter's palette, the poem highlights the power of embracing life's fleeting moments. The bird's eyes, gleaming like gems, invite us to see the world with wonder and love, urging us to rise above the ordinary and live with purpose. In its delicate fragility, the bird teaches a profound lesson: to spread our wings, sing our truth, and savor the beauty that life offers, no matter how brief. A call to celebrate the richness of existence, this poem encourages us to weave our own tapestry of light, embracing each moment with belief and joy.

Frost-Kissed Dreams

In winter's grasp, the world is still,
A hush descends upon the hill.
The air is crisp, the snow is deep,
In peaceful slumber, nature's asleep.

The trees stand bare, branches strong,
As if they've known winter all along.
A silver moon in the midnight sky,
Casts its glow, as the world goes by.

A frosty breath, a shiver's trace,
Yet there's a beauty in this icy space.
In every snowflake, a work of art,
A masterpiece from nature's heart.

Cozy fires and cups of tea,
Warmth and comfort for you and me.
Within winter's grasp, we navigate,
Savor the cold, let dreams take shape.

In the season of snow and frost,
Let's find the beauty that's not lost.
Winter's magic, in its own dance,
Brings a different charm, a subtle trance.

In *Frost-Kissed Dreams*, winter is portrayed not as a harsh season, but as one of peaceful stillness and quiet beauty. Through vivid imagery of snow-covered hills, bare trees, and a silver moon, the poem evokes the serene magic of the cold months. The world's stillness invites reflection, while the delicate snowflakes are seen as masterpieces from nature's heart. The warmth of fires and tea offers solace against the chill, creating a contrast that highlights the comforting charm of the season. Winter's quiet embrace, with its subtle dance of frost and snow, becomes a reminder to find beauty in every moment, even in the stillest times. A perfect addition to a collection that celebrates the seasons, this poem invites readers to embrace the tranquility and magic of winter, urging them to find comfort in the season's frosty dreams and warmth alike.

Lost Time

In the fabric of moments, woven fine,

A thread, delicate design.

Lost time, elusive, slipping away,

A thief stealing the light of day.

In grasp, like grains of sand,

Through fingers slipped, unplanned.

Fleeting, whispers in the wind,

Lost where memories thinned.

Clock ticks, relentless and sly,

Each second, a quiet goodbye.

A phantom, elusive and fleet,

Leaving echoes of bittersweet.

In the garden of hours, seconds bloom,

A shadow, a persistent gloom.

Footprints on the sands of the past,

Fade away, as if they were never cast.

In absence, wisdom may gleam,

Reflection profound, a distant dream.

In loss, the value of moments find,

In time's weave, forever entwined.

Let no regret be the echo's refrain,

Let lessons from lost time remain.

Cherish the moment, in its fleeting grace,

Once gone, no journey can retrace.

Lost Time captures the poignant and inevitable passage of time, using rich imagery to convey its fleeting nature. The poem likens lost moments to slipping grains of sand, evoking a sense of helplessness as time slips away unbidden. Each tick of the clock serves as a quiet goodbye, leaving behind only echoes of what was. Yet, within this loss lies the possibility of wisdom, as reflection on the past offers valuable lessons. The poem encourages readers to cherish every fleeting moment and to embrace the lessons learned from time's ever-vanishing grasp. A powerful reminder to live in the present and savor the grace of now, "Lost Time" resonates with universal truths about the impermanence of life, making it a perfect addition to a collection focused on introspection, growth, and the beauty of the ephemeral.

Ode to Season's Spring

In spring's greetings, the world awakes,

As life from slumber gently breaks.

A burst of color, a fragrant bloom,

Nature's paintbrush, in full costume.

The trees adorn their emerald gown,

And flowers in the meadows crown.

With warming sun and gentle rain,

A symphony of growth, a lively domain.

The birds return with joyful song,

A melody to which we sing along.

In springtime's dance, we find our pose,

And cherish nature's poetic prose.

The days extend, the nights are mild,

In spring's affinity, love is reconciled.

A season of hope, of joy, and cheer,

As springtime whispers, "The world is here."

Let us celebrate the season's birth,

As the Earth renews its precious worth.

In spring's sweet arms, we find our way,

To warmly welcome each and every day.

In *Ode to Season's Spring*, the poet paints a vivid and uplifting portrait of spring's arrival, as nature awakens from winter's slumber and bursts forth in color and vitality. The trees don their emerald gowns, flowers crown the meadows, and the sun and rain create a symphony of growth and renewal. The return of birds singing their joyful melodies ushers in a sense of harmony and celebration. Spring is depicted as a season of hope, love, and reconciliation, inviting readers to cherish the warmth and beauty it brings. The poem is a tender reminder to embrace the season's rebirth and to welcome each day with a renewed sense of wonder and gratitude. Perfect for a collection that celebrates nature's cycles, this ode captures the essence of spring as a time for personal and universal renewal, making it an inspiring and heartfelt addition to any poetry anthology.

Ode to the Sunrise

Ode to the Sunrise, a magical sight,

Bringing warmth and hope with each morning light,

You paint the world with a tender caress,

In your presence, deep feelings we confess.

As you emerge from the horizon's embrace,

The break of day unfurls at a steady pace,

Reminding us of life's sweet, tender care,

Ode to the Sunrise, your glory fills the air.

Your beauty, a beacon, a life-giving spark,

A gift from the heavens to chase away dark,

Waking up the world with a soft, inviting call,

Ode to the Sunrise, we cherish it all.

In the vibrant chorus of birds that sing,

We find the melody that life does bring,

Promising day so bright, lovely, and new,

Ode to the Sunrise, we're thankful for you.

In your golden hues, our spirits take flight,

Ode to the Sunrise, guiding us so bright,

Seizing moments with boundless surprise,

A symbol of life, hope, dreams that arise.

Ode to the Sunrise is a radiant celebration of the dawn, capturing the profound beauty and life-affirming energy of the morning sun. Through vivid imagery, the poem paints the sunrise as a beacon of warmth and hope, gently ushering in a new day with its golden hues. The sunrise is not only a physical phenomenon but also a symbol of renewal and possibility, awakening both the earth and the soul. The chorus of birdsong adds to the melody of life that the sunrise brings, making each moment feel like a gift. The poem invites readers to embrace the promise of each new day, filled with hope, dreams, and the potential for boundless joy. This ode serves as a reminder to cherish the fleeting moments of beauty and the gift of each sunrise, making it a perfect addition to any poetry collection that seeks to inspire and uplift.

Seashores of Serenity

Upon the gentle, white, and sandy shore,
Where waves kiss land with whispers, evermore,
A lesson in serenity unfolds its grace,
In nature's tranquil, vast and boundless space.

The tides that ebb and flow, a constant dance,
Like life's own ups and downs, they enhance,
The beauty of existence, the highs and lows,
Teaching us to accept what life bestows.

The sands beneath our feet, grains so small,
Remind us of time's passage, the grandest of all,
For every grain tells tales of ancient shores,
And every moment lived, a memory to explore.

In shells that line the beach, treasures to find,
A reminder that life's beauty is often entwined,
With moments hidden, waiting to be seen,
Just like the pearls concealed in a shell's sheen.

The seashore teaches patience, acceptance, and grace,
As we gaze into the horizon's endless embrace,
A reminder that life's mysteries will unfurl,
In the serenity of seashore, the wisdom of the world.

In *Seashores of Serenity*, the poet invites readers to experience the tranquil beauty and profound lessons of the beach, where the gentle waves and shifting sands become metaphors for life's ever-changing journey. The ebb and flow of the tides echo the highs and lows that enrich existence, teaching us to embrace all that life bestows. The sands beneath our feet, each grain a reminder of time's passage, offer a poignant reflection on the fleeting nature of moments. The hidden treasures in the shells on the shore symbolize life's concealed beauty, urging us to seek out and appreciate the quiet wonders that often pass unnoticed. The poem calls for patience, acceptance, and grace, inviting us to find wisdom in the serene embrace of nature. With its message of reflection, growth, and the timeless rhythm of life, this poem is a perfect addition to a collection that celebrates the deep, universal truths found in nature's quiet moments, inspiring readers to appreciate the peace and wisdom the world offers.

Shores of Life

Amid the sands where ocean waves embrace,

A timeless tale of life, they do efface.

The beaches whisper secrets to our soul,

In every grain of sand, a story's told.

Beneath the sun's warm, golden, gentle kiss,

Life's complexities, we often dismiss.

The tides, they ebb and flow, just like our days,

Each sunset brings an end in countless ways.

Upon the shores, we find both joy and tears,

As time, like seashells, echoes through the years.

A mirror to our lives, these shores reflect,

The beauty and the trials we collect.

In beaches, we discover life's grand scheme,

A fleeting moment in a boundless dream.

To live with purpose, love, and never cease,

Is to find meaning in the shores of peace.

Let us savor every grain of sand,

As life's expansive beach is where we stand.

Embrace the waves, the sun, the endless sea,

And find the hidden treasures meant to be.

In *Shores of Life*, the poet draws a profound parallel between the ocean's shore and the journey of life itself. The ebb and flow of the tides symbolize the passage of time, while the beach—ever changing, yet constant—reflects the joys and challenges we face. Each grain of sand carries a story, a metaphor for the countless moments that make up our lives. The poem invites readers to embrace life's complexities with purpose and love, finding peace in the fleeting nature of existence. Just as the ocean's waves shape the shore, life's moments—both joyful and sorrowful—shape our hearts. The message is clear: to live fully is to find meaning in both the calm and the storm. With its elegant blend of reflection, acceptance, and timeless wisdom, "Shores of Life" offers readers an inspiring meditation on the beauty and depth of life, making it a perfect addition to any collection focused on finding purpose and meaning.

The Wisdom of Waterfalls

In waterfalls' tumultuous, splendid grace,
We find profound lessons to embrace.
They mirror life's journey, wild and free,
Teaching us what it means to truly be.

As waters plunge from heights so grand,
They tell us to rise when we stumble on land.
In every fall, in each daring leap,
A reminder to rise, to wake from our sleep.

Waterfalls whisper of patience and time,
Their constant carving, a rhythm sublime.
They teach us that greatness isn't rushed,
But in persistence, our dreams are hushed.

Amid the chaos of their crashing song,
We learn that in adversity, we grow strong.
Through obstacles faced, we must persist,
For in challenges, life's lessons exist.

Heed the wisdom that waterfalls share,
In their majestic flow, we find reasons to care.
Through every trial, they stand tall and bright,
Guiding us to navigate life's tumultuous flight.

In *The Wisdom of Waterfalls*, the poet captures the powerful lessons embedded in nature's most dynamic forces, using the waterfall as a metaphor for life's journey. The poem speaks to the importance of persistence, resilience, and patience, drawing parallels between the waterfall's plunge and rise and our own moments of struggle and triumph. It reminds us that true greatness is not hastened but cultivated through steady, unwavering effort. In the face of chaos and adversity, the waterfall teaches us to find strength and purpose, guiding us through life's challenges. The poem's imagery of the waterfall's majestic flow underscores the wisdom we can find in nature, urging readers to embrace each obstacle as a valuable lesson and to navigate life with grace and tenacity. With its powerful message of enduring through hardships, "The Wisdom of Waterfalls" is a perfect addition to a collection that inspires resilience, strength, and growth in the face of life's challenges.

Whispers of the Forests

In forests deep, where shadows play,

A tapestry of existence unfolds each day.

A world of green, a tranquil space,

Where nature imparts its profound grace.

Beneath the canopy, a symphony sings,

From buzzing bees to the eagle's wings.

Each creature, large and small, takes part,

In the intricate dance of nature's art.

The trees, they stand with silent might,

Lessons for us in their steady height.

Rooted deep, they reach for the sky,

Teaching us to stand tall, never shy.

As we wander through the woods so grand,

Let the lessons of the forests expand.

To cherish every moment, joy or strife,

And to embrace the beauty of this life.

In forests deep, we find our way,

Learning from the wisdom they convey.

In every rustle, every whisper of leaves,

A reminder of what it means to truly believe.

In *Whispers of the Forests*, the poet draws readers into the heart of the woods, where the deep, serene beauty of nature reveals its timeless wisdom. Through rich imagery, the poem showcases the forest as a living tapestry, where every creature, from buzzing bees to soaring eagles, participates in the intricate dance of existence. The towering trees, rooted yet reaching for the sky, offer lessons in resilience, strength, and self-assurance, reminding us to stand tall and unwavering. The forest teaches us to embrace every moment, both joyful and challenging, with grace, and to seek the wisdom hidden in nature's whispers. With its message of growth, reflection, and connection to the natural world, "Whispers of the Forests" serves as an inspiring meditation on the beauty of life and the power of nature's lessons. This poem is a perfect addition to any collection focused on the themes of personal growth, wisdom, and the profound beauty of nature.

Whispers of the Wind

Invisible wanderer, swift and free,

The wind, a dancer of eternity,

It whispers secrets through the trees,

Singing ancient songs upon the breeze.

With gentle touch, it strokes the earth,

Caressing every blade of grass from birth,

It paints the sky with clouds that soar,

And whispers tales of lands afar.

In valleys deep, it echoes sighs,

Whispering secrets 'neath the skies,

It carries scents of distant places,

And leaves traces on familiar faces.

Sometimes a gentle, tender kiss,

Or a tempest, raging with bliss,

It molds the landscape with its hands,

Shaping dunes in distant sands.

The wind, a lover, wild and free,

Roaming vast realms, no boundaries see,

In its embrace, we find release,

And in its song, we find our peace.

Let it play its timeless tune,

Beneath the sun, beneath the moon,

For in its whispers, we find our kin,

In the endless dance, where it begins.

In *Whispers of the Wind*, the poet evokes the wind as a mystical, eternal force that moves freely across the world, whispering ancient secrets and shaping the earth. The wind is portrayed as both a gentle lover and a tempestuous spirit, offering a sense of release and peace to those attuned to its presence. Through vivid imagery, the wind paints the sky, carries scents from distant lands, and molds the landscape with its touch, connecting all of nature in a timeless dance. The poem invites readers to listen to the whispers of the wind, finding kinship and peace in its endless journey. With its themes of freedom, connection, and the profound beauty of the natural world, "Whispers of the Wind" serves as a powerful meditation on the invisible forces that shape our lives, making it a perfect addition to a poetry collection that celebrates the beauty, mystery, and unity of nature.

Ephemeral Splendor

In the sky's grand theater, a masterpiece unfolds,

As the sun descends in hues of red and gold.

The world holds its breath, a tranquil hush,

As daylight and darkness softly brush.

The sunset's beauty, a fleeting embrace,

Reflects the essence of life's graceful pace.

In every horizon where the sun takes its flight,

We glimpse the magic of day turning to night.

Each moment, a reminder, as the colors ignite,

That life's beauty is found in its gentle twilight.

Like the sun, we too have our destined descent,

But it's in our journey that true beauty is spent.

Let us cherish each day as the sun takes its bow,

For in life's fleeting moments, our beauty we endow.

Like a sunset, our time is both brief and sublime,

May we shine in existence, through space and time.

In *Ephemeral Splendor*, the poet evokes the profound beauty of the sunset as a metaphor for the transient nature of life. As the sun descends in hues of red and gold, the poem reflects on the delicate balance between day and night, urging readers to recognize the grace found in life's fleeting moments. The sunset's brief but magnificent display serves as a reminder that true beauty lies in the journey, not just the destination. Like the sun, we too experience moments of descent, yet it is in those moments that our true essence shines. The poem invites us to cherish each day as it ends, to live with purpose and appreciation for the precious, ephemeral moments that make up our existence. "Ephemeral Splendor" is a poignant meditation on the delicate nature of time, making it a perfect addition to a poetry collection that celebrates the beauty, fragility, and transience of life.

From Seed to Life

In the quiet earth, a seed is sown,

A tiny spark, where life is yet unknown.

It slumbers below, in darkness' embrace,

Dreaming of the sun, its gentle grace.

With gentle rain, the seed begins to stir,

Awakened by the earth's soft whisper.

Roots unfurl, seeking depths profound,

While above, a tender sprout breaks ground.

The sun bestows its warmth, a golden kiss,

Each ray a promise of springtime bliss.

Leaves unfurl, in a vibrant, verdant hue,

Life's tender essence, born anew.

In seasons' rhythm, the seedling stands proud,

Its growth a symphony, both soft and loud.

Branches stretch, embracing sky and air,

A testament to life's enduring care.

Blossoms bloom, a fragrant, vivid display,

Each petal sings of life's grand array.

From a tiny seed, a miracle has sprung,

A life begun, with songs yet unsung.

In every seed, the promise of tomorrow,
A tale of joy, of love, of pain, and sorrow.
From seed to life, the cycle does repeat,
A sacred dance, profound and bittersweet.

From Seed to Life beautifully captures the timeless journey of growth and transformation, using the metaphor of a seed's life cycle to reflect the stages of human existence. The poem begins in the quiet earth, where a seed lies in darkness, filled with untapped potential, and follows its awakening through rain and sunlight. With each new stage—roots unfurling, leaves blooming, branches reaching—the poem emphasizes the grace of nature's cycles and the miracles of life unfolding. The blossoming of the seed is both a literal and symbolic manifestation of life's continuous rhythm, encompassing both the joys and sorrows that define our existence. The closing lines of the poem speak to the cyclical nature of life itself, a "sacred dance" of growth, loss, and renewal. With its themes of resilience, hope, and the beauty of life's journey, "From Seed to Life" serves as an inspiring meditation on transformation and the profound interconnections between all living things. This poem is a perfect addition to a poetry collection that celebrates the beauty of nature and the cycles of existence.

Whispers in Time's Embrace

Clutching grains of sand as they slip away,

Unplanned, they vanish in a fleeting foray.

Whispers in the wind as memories grow thin,

Lost in the shuffle, where do they all begin?

Time ticks on, each second a sigh,

Quiet goodbyes as moments fly by.

Phantom of the past, elusive yet fleet,

Leaving echoes, both bitter and sweet.

In life's garden, seconds bloom and fade,

Shadows linger, a constant charade.

Footprints lost vanish in the sands of time,

Lost to the wind, like a forgotten rhyme.

Amid absence, wisdom takes its stand,

Reflections deep, like dreams unplanned.

Wisdom from loss, kindness entwined,

Forever bound in life's grand design.

Regrets echo, a haunting refrain,

Lessons learned, from joy and pain.

Cherish each moment, in its fleeting embrace,

For once it's gone, no return to that space.

In *Whispers in Time's Embrace*, the poet delves into the profound and inevitable passage of time, capturing the ephemeral nature of each moment. The poem evokes the image of grains of sand slipping away, symbolizing how memories and experiences fade, leaving behind only whispers in the wind. Time ticks on relentlessly, and the echoes of the past, both bitter and sweet, linger like forgotten rhymes. The garden of life blooms and withers in a delicate dance of shadows and light, reminding us of the fleetingness of existence. Through this meditation on loss, regret, and reflection, the poem reveals the wisdom that arises from embracing time's transience. The closing message urges readers to cherish every moment, as once passed, they cannot be retrieved. With its poignant themes of mortality, wisdom, and the beauty of impermanence, "Whispers in Time's Embrace" serves as a powerful reflection on the human experience, making it a perfect addition to a collection that explores the passage of time, the lessons of life, and the profound beauty found in life's fleeting moments.

Rock Solid Wisdom

In valleys deep and mountains high,

Where ancient whispers softly sigh,

Amid the streams and fields of green,

Lies a truth, serene, unseen.

They stand through time's embrace,

With strength and calm upon their face,

A silent guide through life's unknown,

They teach us how to be alone.

Their surfaces, both rough and smooth,

A testament to time's own groove,

Weathered by the storm's harsh kiss,

Yet holding secrets deep in bliss.

In shadows cast by moonlit night,

Or bathed in dawn's first gentle light,

They anchor souls in search of peace,

From worldly chains, they find release.

When life is fraught with storms and fears,

And paths are blurred by doubtful tears,

Look to the rock, so firm, so true,

For guidance in what you should do.

Embrace the strength, the calm, the grace,

Let steadfast love your fears erase,

For in the rocks, both great and small,

Lies wisdom that can heal us all.

In *Rock Solid Wisdom*, the poet explores the enduring power and quiet wisdom of nature's rock formations as a metaphor for strength, resilience, and peace. Through vivid imagery of ancient rocks in valleys and mountains, the poem conveys the rock's ability to endure through time, weathering life's storms while remaining steadfast and unbroken. The rocks stand as silent guides, offering solace and wisdom in the face of life's uncertainties. Their surfaces, both rough and smooth, symbolize the complexity of life's challenges and the grace found in accepting them. The poem invites readers to seek solace in these natural pillars, urging them to find peace, strength, and guidance in moments of fear or doubt. By embracing the rock's enduring wisdom, we can release our worldly burdens and discover healing. "Rock Solid Wisdom" serves as a powerful reminder of the quiet strength that lies within nature—and within ourselves—making it a poignant and inspirational addition to any poetry collection.

The Flower of Life

In the garden of eternity, where mysteries entwine,

There blooms a flower of life, a symbol so divine.

Its petals whisper secrets, of cycles ever-turning,

Of creation's dance with death, of endless stars' yearning.

In each delicate fold, the sacred masculine resides,

Strength and power intertwined, where cosmic forces abide.

Yet nestled in between, the divine feminine's grace,

Nurturing, birthing life, in an ever-changing embrace.

Within the heart of the flower, a cosmic web is spun,

Binding souls together, under the eternal sun.

Each petal a universe, where galaxies unfurl,

Connecting every being, in the grand cosmic swirl.

Through cycles of birth and death, the flower tells its tale,

Of how endings are beginnings, in life's eternal trail.

It holds within its essence, the key to hidden lore,

Unraveling time's mysteries, as it opens every door.

Within its sacred geometry, the secrets of the stars,

Echo whispers of creation, from near and distant bars.

The unity of existence, in every intricate line,

Bridges the gap between mortal and divine.

Let us heed its message, as we journey through this dance,
Embracing life's cycles, in each fleeting circumstance.
For in the flower of life, we find the truth so rare,
That creation and wisdom, bound in love and care.

In *The Flower of Life*, the poet delves into the profound interconnectedness of existence, using the image of the flower as a symbol of creation, wisdom, and the cyclical nature of life. The flower's petals, representing both the sacred masculine and feminine, embody the balance of strength and nurturing, power and grace that govern the universe. The poem weaves a cosmic tapestry where each petal mirrors a universe, revealing the endless dance between birth and death. Through its sacred geometry, the flower invites us to explore the mysteries of time, space, and the deep unity that binds all beings under the eternal sun. It teaches that life's cycles—though filled with endings—are also filled with new beginnings, emphasizing that wisdom and love reside at the heart of creation. "The Flower of Life" offers a beautiful reminder that the secrets of existence, both cosmic and personal, are rooted in love and care, encouraging readers to embrace the sacred dance of life in all its fleeting moments. This poem, rich in spiritual and philosophical depth, would be a powerful and transformative addition to a poetry collection focused on life's profound truths.

The Fruit of Life

In this cosmic dance of existence's weave,

We grasp the Fruit of Life, our hearts receive.

Thirteen truths embodied, each with its own tale,

A journey of souls, in love's ever-present gale.

Within Truth's domain, clarity's bright beam,

Guiding our steps through each fleeting dream.

In Self-love's embrace, a haven so pure,

Where scars transform to stories, strong and sure.

Acceptance's melody, a soft, soothing tune,

Embracing our flaws, under a gentle moon.

Beauty's palette paints, in colors divine,

Whispering tales of grace in every heart's line.

Knowledge's quest, an endless, eager chase,

Wisdom's whispers, in life's sacred space.

Wellness blooms freely, in life's joyful dance,

Harmonizing with fate, in its rhythmic trance.

Wholeness unfolds, a mosaic so fine,

Unity's embrace, where souls intertwine.

Strength's steadfast rise, through trials untold,

Resilient spirits, in stories of old.

Divinity whispers in silence profound,

A connection eternal, love's sweet rebound.

Clarity's beacon shines, in moments so clear,

Illuminating paths, dispelling all fear.

Empowerment's fire, ignites deep within,

Dreams take flight, where new worlds begin.

Freedom's sweet song, in the winds of the night,

Savoring life's moments, in purest delight.

In the intricate design of the universe,

Let us embrace each fruit, as treasures immerse.

The thirteen fruits of life, a story yet begun,

The essence of existence, in unity spun.

The Fruit of Life is a profound and intricate exploration of thirteen transformative truths that encompass the core of human existence. Through the metaphor of fruit, the poet encapsulates the wisdom we glean from embracing life's complexities. Each "fruit" represents a powerful force— clarity, self-love, acceptance, beauty, knowledge, wellness, wholeness, unity, strength, divinity, empowerment, and freedom—guiding us through our cosmic dance. The poem highlights the importance of self-love, inner strength, and the pursuit of wisdom as we navigate life's journey. Each line beautifully interweaves the concept of divine connection and empowerment, portraying how each truth shapes and sustains the soul. With striking imagery and lyrical depth, "The Fruit of Life" invites readers to reflect on their own journey, recognizing that the essence of life is found in the embrace of love, clarity, and freedom. This poem is a celebration of life's profound truths, offering wisdom, guidance, and a gentle invitation to live in harmony with the universe's divine design. Its spiritual depth and evocative imagery make it a compelling piece for a poetry collection focused on growth, transformation, and unity.

The Ocean's Eternal Symphony

Where sun and sea in union meet,
Lies a realm both wild and sweet,
An endless waltz, a timeless tale,
Nature's hymn, where hearts set sail.

Beneath the azure, secrets hide,
Where gentle giants silently glide,
Coral gardens, with hues so bright,
Whisper wonders in the silent night.

Moon's soft caress on tranquil waves,
Reflects a beauty, the ocean craves,
Stars above and stars below,
In mirrored depths, their stories flow.

The sea's embrace, a balm so kind,
Heals the wounds of heart and mind,
Its melody, a soothing choir,
Stills the storms with tranquil fire.

In every crest, a prayer is heard,
For those who wander, soul unblurred,
A timeless bond, ancient and deep,
The ocean's promise, forever to keep.

With each gentle tide's rhythmic swell,

Our souls entwined, in its spell,

In the symphony of life's grand design,

The ocean's heartbeat, yours and mine.

The Ocean's Eternal Symphony explores the profound, healing relationship between the ocean and the human soul. With imagery of gentle giants, coral gardens, and the celestial dance of stars above and below, the poem speaks to the timeless beauty of the sea. It offers solace and serenity, illustrating how nature's endless rhythm can soothe the heart and mind. As the tides ebb and flow, the ocean's melody becomes a balm for the spirit, a reminder of the deep, ancient bond that connects us to the earth. Through its tranquil verses, the poem invites readers to surrender to nature's embrace, finding peace in the eternal harmony of the sea.

The Seed of Life

In realms of thought and cosmic design,
The Seed of Life, a symbol so divine.
Seven circles, in harmony combined,
Tale of the Divine, in patterns entwined.

Within its form, secrets reside,
Unity's essence, where paths coincide.
The cosmic weaver, spinning galaxies wide,
The universe abides, in mystery's guide.

It represents beginnings, fresh and new,
Potential vast, in every view.
A symbol of life, in cycles true,
Eternal truth, in essence to pursue.

Expansion blooms in circular grace,
The universe's heartbeat, in cosmic race.
Infinite paths, where dreams find their place,
Mystery's base, in cosmic embrace.

Harmony's dance in circles untold,
Unity's song, in wisdom's hold.
Interconnected, stories unfold,
Wonders bold, in tales retold.

Cycles of birth and death entwine,

Eternal rhythms, in life's design.

A journey of the soul, in circles divine,

Symbol sublime, in cosmic shine.

In enlightenment's grasp, its meaning clear,

Ancient knowledge, we revere.

Eternity's echo, ever near and dear,

Visions sincere, in wisdom's sphere.

The Seed of Life speaks to the divine symmetry of the universe, using the symbolism of seven interconnected circles to explore unity, creation, and the cycles of existence. It paints a picture of life as a vast cosmic dance, where beginnings and endings flow into one another in an endless rhythm. The seed represents boundless potential, with every path it takes leading to new possibilities. The poem's emphasis on expansion, interconnectedness, and harmony invites readers to reflect on the profound wisdom woven into the fabric of life and the universe. In its graceful verses, the poem offers a timeless meditation on the nature of existence and enlightenment, reminding us of the divine order that guides our journeys.

The Tree of Life

In the heart of ancient woods, a sacred tree,
The Tree of Life, where souls roam free,
Its roots delve deep, in earth's warm hold,
A symbol of the human race, both young and old.

With branches stretching to the celestial skies,
It whispers secrets, of the old and wise,
Each leaf a tale of life's enchanted dance,
In every twist and turn, a mystical trance.

From a tiny seed, tender sprout to sturdy oak,
Mirroring dreams and hopes that we invoke,
A journey shared with both foe and friend,
A dance of change, rebirth that never ends.

In every leaf, life's melody, a story bold,
Of love's embrace, of partings cold,
Yet in its arms, beneath the shades of green,
We find solace, a haven serene.

Let us discover our worth beneath its boughs,
Amidst the whispers of secrets and vows,
For in the Tree of Life, a profound beauty lies,
A thread binding souls, under starlit skies.

The Tree of Life stands as a powerful symbol of growth, connection, and wisdom. Rooted deep in the earth, it represents the shared journey of humanity, from childhood to old age. The tree's expansive branches, reaching toward the heavens, hold the secrets of existence, inviting reflection on the cycles of life, love, and loss. Through its leaves, the poem weaves a melody of shared stories and transformations, showing how each twist and turn in our lives shapes us. Beneath its canopy, we find peace and meaning, a sanctuary where our souls can be nourished. Ultimately, the tree serves as a reminder of our interconnectedness, our enduring beauty, and the timeless bond that unites us all under the vast sky.

Secrets of the Wind

With gentle touch, it strokes the earth's embrace,

Caressing every blade of life's first trace,

It paints the canvas of the sky that soars,

And whispers tales of realms beyond closed doors.

In valleys deep, it echoes our heartfelt sighs,

Whispering secrets under boundless skies,

It carries scents of distant, dream-kissed places,

And leaves its whispered traces on familiar faces.

Sometimes a gentle, tender, timeless kiss,

Or a tempest, raging with untamed bliss,

It sculpts the landscape with its unseen hands,

Shaping dunes in far-off, shifting sands.

The wind, a lover, wild and ever free,

Roaming vast realms, embracing infinity,

In its soft caress, we find our sweet release,

And in its song, we find our deepest peace.

Let it play its eternal, whispered tune,

Beneath the golden sun, beneath the silver moon,

For in its whispers, we find our kindred souls,

In the timeless dance where the universe unfolds.

Secrets of the Wind explores the wind as both a nurturing force and a wild, untamable spirit that carries the wisdom of the earth. It moves through valleys, shapes the world, and whispers secrets of distant realms. In its caress, the wind evokes a sense of release and peace, guiding us on a journey of self-discovery and connection. The poem reflects the wind's ability to transcend boundaries, offering us a sense of unity with all things. Whether gentle or fierce, the wind is portrayed as a timeless, eternal companion—always present, always shaping, always calling us to listen closely to the universe's hidden messages.

Wings of Courage

In the boundless skies, dreams take flight,
A noble eagle, a symbol shining bright.
Wings outstretched, a dance with the breeze,
A journey unfolds, with such elegant ease.

Above the peaks, where aspirations reside,
The eagle soars, life's challenges to confide.
Its keen eyes gaze through the canvas of blue,
A reflection of strength, an emblem true.

Through stormy tempests and winds that assail,
The eagle persists, an unwavering trail.
Resilient feathers, kissed by the gale,
A metaphor for the stories life entails.

In your journey, through highs and lows,
Let your spirit ascend, true essence compose.
Embrace each challenge, each twist, each turn,
In the eagle's flight, let your wisdom burn.

With wings of courage, navigate the unknown,
Rise above troubles, let your strength be shown.
In life's vast expanse, embrace the light,
A symphony written in the eagle's flight.

Wings of Courage is an inspiring poem that captures the essence of resilience and self-discovery through the powerful imagery of an eagle in flight. The poem serves as a poignant reminder of life's challenges, encouraging readers to rise above obstacles with unwavering strength and grace. The eagle, symbolizing freedom and tenacity, guides us through stormy times, offering a compelling vision of perseverance and triumph. This piece not only uplifts the spirit but also encourages personal growth, urging readers to embrace their inner strength and soar toward their dreams with courage and wisdom. The seamless blend of nature's majesty with profound life lessons makes it a deeply resonant and motivational work, perfect for anyone seeking inspiration on their own journey of empowerment.

Chapter Four

The Poetic Odyssey of the Resilient Souls of Haiti

Haiti's Resilient Souls invites readers into the heart of a nation where strength, endurance, and an unbreakable spirit converge. This powerful collection of poems is a tribute to the indomitable courage of the Haitian people—whose tales of struggle, survival, and triumph echo through history. Rich in culture, deeply rooted in tradition, and bound by a shared sense of hope, Haiti has weathered countless storms, yet its essence remains vibrant, a beacon of resilience and unwavering spirit.

Each poem in this collection is a window into the soul of Haiti—offering a vivid tapestry of its landscapes, music, and people. Through themes of love, loss, perseverance, and renewal, readers will feel Haiti's heartbeat in the rhythmic pulse of its life. From the lively energy of the markets to the profound beauty of its natural scenery, Haiti's enduring spirit shines through every verse. The collection captures the voices of revolution, the strength of community, and the hope that transcends even the darkest of times.

In these pages, Haiti's story is told through the lens of duality—where joy and sorrow intertwine, creating a complex yet inspiring narrative. The poems celebrate the rich cultural heritage and identity shaped by centuries of struggle and triumph, highlighting the enduring power of family, unity, and the will to rise again. The strength of the Haitian people is mirrored in each verse, where the power of resilience, love, and hope resonates deeply with anyone who has ever faced adversity.

As you journey through these lines, may you feel the pulse of Haiti—the laughter of children, the whispers of ancestors, and the songs of survival sung against the backdrop of a nation's unyielding determination. These poems remind us that even in our darkest hours, there is always a spark of light, a testament to the power of hope and the strength we all carry within.

Haiti's Resilient Souls is more than a collection of poems—it is a celebration of the human spirit, a call to honor the stories that shape our world, and an invitation to recognize the profound connections that unite us all. In these verses, we discover the enduring strength of our souls, the bonds that transcend time and place, and the shared journey toward healing, hope, and resilience.

Haiti's Resilient Souls

In Port-au-Prince's maze, where shadows writhe and weep,

Kenyan peacekeepers tread, their vows etched soul-deep,

From lands afar they've journeyed, to quell tempest's wrath,

In alleys etched by sorrow, they forge a hopeful path.

A symphony of youth erupts, a clarion call so bright,

The Premier's promise echoes on Youth Day's hallowed light,

To spirits restless, yearning, futures veiled and lean,

They sow their aspirations where despair reigned supreme.

Earth, though weary, embraces each seed with tender might,

In hands weathered by seasons, hope defies the blight,

Beneath skies of burnished silver, they labor and they pray,

For peace to bloom like flamboyants heralding a new day.

In once-bustling markets, now hushed by time's cruel hand,

Whispered dreams are bartered for a kinder, gentler land,

While art adorns the remnants, a palette fierce and bold,

Haiti's undying spirit in azure and in gold.

Vodou drums resound, from peak to verdant vale,

Ancestral wisdom pulses through each rhythmic tale,

In syncopated heartbeats, a nation's soul revives,

Resilience etched in melody, as Haiti thrives.

From Cap-Haïtien's fortress to Jacmel's artisan shore,

The land itself bears witness to trials faced before,

In every Kreyòl proverb, each legend long retold,

The seeds of transformation relentlessly unfold.

For every soldier's vigil, every farmer's toiling hand,

Haiti's essence deepens, rooted in this hallowed land,

United in their struggle, unbowed by history's might,

They forge ahead together, through darkness into light.

Citadelle Laferrière stands, a testament of stone,

To Haitian strength unyielding, a will to stand alone,

Yet in communion gather, the diaspora's embrace,

A global Haitian heart that time cannot erase.

So let the world bear witness to this tapestry of life,

Where joy and sorrow mingle, transcending earthly strife,

For in the soul of Haiti, where freedom's bell still tolls,

A nation rises, phoenix-like, with faith that makes it whole.

From mangoes sweet in Artibonite to Port-au-Prince's core,

The spirit of Toussaint whispers of liberties in store,

Through every trial and triumph, each tear and joyous song,

Haiti endures, unbroken—in unity, strong.

*Haiti's Resilient Soul*s is an evocative and stirring poem that portrays the heart and soul of Haiti, a nation marked by both hardship and extraordinary resilience. Through poignant imagery and rich cultural references, the poem explores the unyielding spirit of Haiti's people—from the efforts of foreign peacekeepers to the enduring strength of farmers and artisans. The poem celebrates Haiti's rich history, its vibrant culture, and the transformative power of unity. Drawing from ancestral wisdom and the timeless legacy of revolution, it portrays Haiti as a nation continually rising above adversity with an unwavering sense of hope and pride. Each verse serves as a testament to the strength of its people, the beauty of their culture, and the profound spirit of survival and renewal that continues to define the Haitian identity. This poem is a powerful tribute to Haiti's past, present, and future, resonating deeply with readers who seek inspiration in resilience, unity, and the enduring power of hope.

A Plea for Haiti

In Haiti's spirited, troubled lands,

A story unfolds, hearts in hands,

Where sorrow's melody fills the air,

And dreams are lost in deep despair.

Beneath the burning sun's harsh glare,

Hopes crumble, burdens too much to bear,

Politics, a wild, relentless tide,

Crushing dreams, where fears reside.

The cries at night, so raw and clear,

In shadows deep, where truths appear,

Promises fade like whispers in the dark,

Leaving hearts empty, searching for a spark.

Amidst this grim and daunting test,

A spark of hope, a welcomed guest,

Hearts entwined in hardship's grasp,

Facing odds, their spirits clasp.

In Haiti's streets, voices rise,

Echoes of freedom, reaching the skies,

Through trials deep, they stand as one,

In chaos' face, their bond is spun.

With courage bold, they face the storm,

Their resilience, a powerful form,

In their eyes, a fire burns bright,

Breaking chains, embracing what's right.

Let us listen to Haiti's call,

A plea for justice, heard by all,

In their fight, we find the key,

Unity's strength, humanity's plea.

A Plea for Haiti the poem powerfully conveys the deep struggles of a nation caught between despair and the unrelenting pursuit of hope. Through vivid imagery, it captures the harsh realities of Haiti's political and social challenges, where dreams are stifled, and the cries for justice echo through the streets. Despite the overwhelming darkness, the poem highlights the unwavering resilience of Haiti's people, who, united in their fight, remain steadfast in their quest for justice, freedom, and equality. With themes of unity, courage, and the enduring human spirit, this poem serves as both a plea for global awareness and a celebration of the strength that binds the Haitian people together. It speaks to the universal need for empathy and action, urging readers to listen, support, and stand with those who face adversity with unyielding determination. This heartfelt call for justice resonates deeply, inspiring both reflection and a collective commitment to making a difference.

A Tribute to Jean-Jacques Dessalines

In the heart of Haiti, a hero bold,

Jean-Jacques Dessalines, his tales untold.

With dreams and hopes, a mortal's plight,

He reached for stars in freedom's radiant light.

From slavery's chains, he carved a way,

A beacon shining in night's gentle sway.

Through tears and laughter, joy and strife,

He lived an epic tale, vibrant with life.

Amidst the turmoil, hope's flame did burn,

His courage in each soul, a lesson to learn.

Through battles fought, and wounds that mend,

He stood for justice that never found end.

In Haiti's cry, he heard the plea,

To rise, unite, and set his people free.

With rebellious heartbeat, a nation's birth,

A spirit fierce, unchained on Earth.

His saga sings of human grace,

In every challenge, love's enduring embrace.

His legacy endures in memory's core,

A spirit noble, cherished forevermore.

A timeless guide in history's glance,

An echo in the universe's endless dance.

For freedom's light, he dreamed a dream,

A guiding star, a hopeful gleam.

In Haiti's weary soul, his spirit dwells,

Through ages past, where strength compels.

A hero's journey, bold and true,

In this heartfelt ode, I honor you.

A Tribute to Jean-Jacques Dessalines the poem eloquently commemorates the life and legacy of one of Haiti's greatest leaders, whose courage and vision carved the path to freedom. Through rich, evocative imagery, it honors Dessalines as a beacon of resilience, a hero who rose from the shackles of slavery to become a symbol of justice and liberation. His battle for Haiti's independence is framed as a timeless saga of hope, strength, and unity, embodying the unbreakable spirit of the Haitian people. The poem captures the enduring influence of his spirit, which continues to inspire generations, reminding us that his fight for freedom and dignity is not only a chapter in history but a living, breathing force that continues to shape the world. This heartfelt tribute offers both reverence and reflection, making it a powerful addition to any collection focused on courage, justice, and the enduring fight for liberty.

An Afro-Haitian Odyssey

Where azure waves caress the golden shore,

And tropic breezes whisper ancient lore,

Afro-Haitian hearts, like molten ore,

Forge freedom's anthem forevermore.

Beneath the ceiba's sprawling, sacred arms,

Their stories weave a tapestry of charms,

In konpa rhythms and vodou's mystic balms,

A spirit dance that soothes and alarms.

From Cap-Haïtien's streets to Jacmel's doors,

Where Citadelle Laferrière proudly soars,

The echo of Toussaint's dream still roars,

A history that time itself adores.

In veins, the blood of Guinean kings still flows,

With memories of baobabs and indigos,

Yet on this isle, a new world's garden grows,

Where freedom's flower eternally glows.

Through fields of sugarcane and coffee groves,

Where once the chains of bondage cruelly wove,

Now stand the free, their hearts a treasure trove

Of courage that no tyrant can remove.

In marketplaces bright with madras hues,

And mountain paths where mist obscures the views,

The strength of ancestors forever fuses

With every step that freedom chooses.

They break oppression's yoke and proudly sing

Of Haiti's glory, let their voices ring

Across the Caribbean, on freedom's wing,

A phoenix nation, ever-flourishing.

From Ayiti's soil, resilience blooms anew,

A legacy of hope, both old and true,

In every Kreyòl proverb, in every hue

Of art that paints their world in vibrant blue.

An Afro-Haitian Odyssey is an eloquent and dynamic tribute to the soul of Haiti, where the fusion of African heritage and revolutionary spirit comes alive. Through vivid imagery and powerful metaphors, the poem explores the deeply rooted history of Haiti's Afro-Haitian people, celebrating their resilience, cultural richness, and unyielding pursuit of freedom. From the echoes of Toussaint Louverture's dream to the vibrant landscapes and rhythms that define the nation, this poem encapsulates the timeless strength of Haiti's people. It evokes the profound connection between their past and present, with each verse serving as a tribute to their enduring legacy of courage and hope. With themes of freedom, unity, and cultural pride, the poem speaks to the heart of every reader, highlighting Haiti's triumphant spirit as a beacon of liberty and strength for all nations. This work transcends the borders of history, offering a universal message of perseverance, pride, and the transformative power of heritage.

Capois La-Mort: The Lion of Vertières

In Haiti's heart, where freedom's flame

Did spark against a tyrant's claim,

A hero emerged, valiant and bold,

His bravery and legacy in legends told.

François Capois, a name revered,

In battle's storm, he never feared.

With steadfast heart and courage bright,

He led his troop into the fatal fight.

At Vertières, the fateful field,

Where Haitian souls refused to yield,

Through gunfire's roar and cannon's blast,

Capois marched on, flag held fast.

His horse beneath him met its end,

Yet Capois defiantly rose, a foe to rend.

"Forward!" he cried, "We shall not fall,

Freedom or death, we give our all!"

The French, in awe, their shots in vain,

Could not subdue this lion's reign.

Capois La-Mort, resolute and undeterred,

Became freedom's enduring guiding word.

With every step, he carved a path,

Through history's storm, battle's wrath.

At dawn in Haiti, with freedom's might,

Won by heroes in their relentless fight.

In battle's heart, with courage pure,

Capois La-Mort, in perpetuity sure.

A hero's name, a timeless tale of pride,

His unyielding spirit always by our side.

François Capois, your name forever engraved,

In hearts of those who the path have braved.

With courage, honor, steadfast and true,

In every endeavor, we proudly honor you.

In Haiti's land, where valor finds its stand,

Your spirit leads our steadfast command.

For freedom's cause, we rise once more,

Inspired by you, the brave, Capois La-Mort.

Capois La-Mort: The Lion of Vertières is a poignant and stirring tribute to one of Haiti's most iconic heroes, François Capois, whose unparalleled bravery at the Battle of Vertières cemented his place in history as a symbol of freedom and resilience. The poem paints a vivid, heroic picture of Capois, who, despite facing insurmountable odds, led his troops with unwavering courage in their fight for independence. His relentless spirit in the face of death and his resolute defiance against tyranny make him an enduring symbol of Haiti's struggle for liberty. The poem's themes of courage, sacrifice, and honor resonate deeply, offering a powerful tribute to not only Capois's legacy but also the enduring spirit of Haiti's people. Through its evocative imagery and compelling narrative, this poem captures the essence of freedom's fight, making it a timeless call to honor those who rise against oppression. With its universal message of bravery and unyielding strength, it is an inspiring homage to the heroism that shaped Haiti and continues to inspire generations today.

Charlemagne Péralte

In Haiti, where freedom's fire burned,

A hero rose as daylight to shadow turned.

Born in Hinche in eighteen eighty-six,

Charlemagne Péralte, with resolve to fix.

A lieutenant first, loyal and true,

Disillusioned by the foreign hue.

The U.S. occupation, harsh and stark,

Made him doubt, ignited a spark.

In nineteen eighteen, in the Cacos' lead,

A bold uprising, where valor took heed.

To expel foreign forces, fierce and grand,

Reclaim sovereignty, Haiti's sacred land.

Through mountains high and valleys wide,

His leadership and heart, a nation's pride.

The Haitian people rallied to his call,

In Péralte's name, they stood tall.

Captured by the foe in nineteen nineteen,

His life was taken, yet his spirit keen.

Though his death was a significant blow,

His legacy still continues to grow.

Péralte, a true hero in the strife,

Inspires generations with his life.

A national hero, in hearts he stays,

Haiti honors him in countless ways.

His story, a torch that guides us still,

In every heart, it echoes with goodwill.

Charlemagne Péralte, a timeless beacon,

A hero's light that never weakens.

Charlemagne Péralte is a compelling and evocative tribute to one of Haiti's most revered heroes, whose defiant stand against foreign occupation became a symbol of national pride and resistance. The poem vividly captures the rise of Péralte from a loyal soldier to the leader of the Cacos, as he rallied his people to reclaim their sovereignty in the face of overwhelming odds. Through his courage, sacrifice, and unbreakable commitment to Haiti's freedom, Péralte's legacy transcends his untimely death, inspiring generations with his unwavering dedication to justice and independence. The poem resonates with themes of leadership, resistance, and the enduring power of hope, making it a powerful tribute to the enduring spirit of Haiti's fight for sovereignty. Through its poignant portrayal of Péralte's heroism, the poem immortalizes his story as a timeless source of inspiration, urging readers to honor the sacrifices made for liberty and the power of unity in the face of adversity.

Claudinette Fouchard

In Port-au-Prince, where stars softly gleam,

A maiden was born to fulfill a dream.

Claudinette Fouchard, with beauty rare,

Grace and poise beyond compare.

Her eyes, deep pools of Caribbean blue,

Held secrets of lands she traveled through.

Educated in Paris, standing tall,

A beacon of wisdom, inspiring all.

Fluent in tongues, six voices she spoke,

Each word a bridge, a bond unbroke.

From France to Greece, her footsteps traced,

In every place, her spirit embraced.

At twenty-one, with beauty so grand,

She won the crown in a distant land.

"World Sugar Queen," they hailed her name,

A title rare, a golden flame.

With modesty and simple grace,

She represented Haiti, her native place.

The Black Pearl, they called her true,

A radiant gem the world once knew.

Beyond the titles and global fame,

Lies a story with depth, untamed.

A woman of strength, of passion and fire,

Whose life and legacy inspire.

Her path was not always smooth or straight,

She faced her trials, embraced her fate.

With resilience and courage, she forged her way,

A symbol of hope, still shining today.

Let us remember Claudinette's name,

A legend of beauty, forever in fame.

For in her story, young girls can see,

A dream fulfilled, a destiny free.

Claudinette Fouchard is an empowering and inspiring poem that honors the life of a trailblazing Haitian woman who became a global icon. From her humble beginnings in Port-au-Prince to her rise as the "World Sugar Queen" and a symbol of elegance and intellect, the poem captures Claudinette's essence as a beacon of hope and resilience. Fluent in six languages and celebrated worldwide, her story exemplifies the power of education, grace, and determination. Her legacy goes beyond beauty, representing strength, courage, and the limitless potential of women to achieve greatness. The poem serves as both a tribute to her legacy and an inspiration for young girls everywhere, reminding them that with resilience and passion, any dream is possible. Through its powerful portrayal of Claudinette's life and impact, this poem resonates with readers seeking empowerment, cultural pride, and the celebration of women who redefine boundaries.

Abdaraya Toya "Victoria Montou"

In Dahomey's ancient, verdant hold,
An Amazon princess, with a heart so bold,
A warrior fierce, with spirit's might,
Stood as an angel in heavenly light.

Her braided mane, a regal crown,
Flowing like the Nile, wild and renowned,
Her skin adorned with earth's warm embrace,
Reflecting strength and boundless grace.

With eyes that pierced the shadowed veil,
With a gaze fierce yet tender, she set sail,
Her voice, a hymn of ancient lore,
Resounding through the forest's core.

In Haiti's revolution, her spirit soared,
Each strike a poetic flare, power roared,
Leading with wisdom, strength, and fire,
A beacon of her people's hearts' desire.

Within her seat of passion, a melody sweet,
Love's fifth harmony, a soft retreat,
A princess fearless, her kindness true,
In her, the world's great beauty grew.

In quiet moments, by moon's soft glow,

She sought solace, her heart a gentle flow,

Amidst the silence, her spirit rose,

A warrior's grace, eternally composed.

Sing of Abdaraya Toya in legend's lore,

This Amazon of Dahomey, evermore,

A tale of timeless strength and harmony,

A star enlightened, our hearts' symphony.

Abdaraya Toya 'Victoria Montou' is an evocative and empowering poem that immortalizes the spirit of an extraordinary Amazonian warrior from Dahomey, whose fierce leadership and unwavering resolve contributed to Haiti's revolution. This poem beautifully intertwines themes of strength, grace, and wisdom, capturing the essence of a woman who was both a warrior and a symbol of love and harmony. Her presence is described as powerful yet tender, a reflection of her dual role as both a leader in battle and a keeper of peace. Through her unbreakable resolve and the beauty of her spirit, the poem offers an inspiring portrayal of a woman whose legacy transcends her time. Her story becomes a timeless source of inspiration, illustrating the profound impact of women warriors who forge paths of freedom, strength, and unity. Through poetic imagery and deep emotion, this tribute serves as a celebration of resilience, leadership, and the power of the feminine spirit in shaping history.

Dutty Boukman: The Fire of Rebellion

In Saint-Domingue's shadowed night,

Where stars blinked down on fields of plight,

A voice arose, both fierce and bright,

To lead the way, to stand and fight.

Dutty Boukman, with spirit bold,

A legend in the stories told,

His heart aflame, his mission gold,

The seeds of revolution sowed.

At Bois Caïman, the sacred grove,

Where whispers of rebellion rove,

He called the spirits, strength they wove,

A pact for freedom, hearts to move.

A priest, a leader, eyes ablaze,

He spoke of being free from slavery's gaze,

In unity, their spirits raised,

To break from oppression's darkest days.

With drums of war and chants of fire,

They sparked a nation's great desire,

To rise against their lowly mire,

For freedom's cause, they'd never tire.

Boukman's name, a radiant flame,

In the darkest night, his guiding aim,

His courage lent the slaves their claim,

Turning tears to stars, a celestial frame.

In Haiti's heart, his spirit thrives,

In every breath, his legend dives,

For Dutty Boukman's call survives,

In every soul that freedom drives.

Dutty Boukman: The Fire of Rebellion is a stirring and evocative poem that immortalizes the legendary Haitian leader, Dutty Boukman, whose call to arms sparked the Haitian Revolution. Through powerful imagery and lyrical grace, the poem brings to life Boukman's vision of freedom and unity, particularly during the iconic Bois Caïman ceremony where he united enslaved people through spiritual and cultural strength. His fiery determination and bold leadership are captured as a beacon of resistance and empowerment, lighting the path toward liberation. The poem not only honors Boukman's role in Haiti's revolutionary history but also celebrates the enduring power of freedom and rebellion. It portrays him as both a spiritual and revolutionary figure whose courage continues to resonate in the fight for justice and equality. This tribute offers a timeless, profound reflection on the resilience of oppressed people and the enduring impact of leaders who challenge tyranny.

The Citadelle Laferrière

In Haiti's wild embrace, a fortress stands tall,
A symbol of dreams, a beacon for all.
The Citadelle Laferrière, crowned by mountains bold,
Where freedom's song forever unfolds.

Born from the flames of revolution's fight,
Its walls whisper tales of courage and might.
Henri Christophe's dream, noble and grand,
A fortress of hope in our Haitian land.

From chains and sorrow, a nation did rise,
Defying the odds with bright, hopeful eyes.
Stone by stone, with sweat and tears,
A testament strong through the passing years.

High on Bonnet-à-L'Eveque's lush green domain,
A UNESCO gem, history's proud chain.
Guardian of liberty, against darkness it stands,
A monument cherished, built by loving hands.

Beyond mere stone and mortar, it holds our soul,
A people's unity, a timeless goal.
Henri's legacy, deep in our heart's ground,
A dream that lives on, in freedom's sound.

Let us remember, in the Citadelle's grace,

The spirit that binds us, in every embrace.

For in its towering walls, we find the key,

To our Haitian spirit, forever free.

The Citadelle Laferrière is an evocative and majestic poem that honors one of Haiti's most powerful symbols of independence and national pride. With lyrical beauty and historical depth, the poem transports readers to the heart of Haiti's revolutionary past, celebrating the Citadelle Laferrière as both a physical and spiritual monument to freedom. Built by Henri Christophe after Haiti's successful revolution, this fortress represents the unity, strength, and unwavering spirit of the Haitian people. The poem intertwines the Citadelle's stone walls with the profound legacy of resistance and liberty, offering readers an inspiring reflection on the sacrifices made for freedom and the enduring power of hope. A perfect blend of history and poetry, The Citadelle Laferrière invites readers to connect with Haiti's rich heritage and the universal ideals of courage, unity, and self-determination.

Henri Christophe: The Defender of the Faith

From chains of iron to freedom's light,

Henri rose to lead in Haiti's fight.

With courage fierce and heart aflame,

He carved his path, earned his name.

Through revolution's fervent blaze,

He stood with Toussaint in those days.

And with Dessalines, side by side,

For freedom's dream, they fought with pride.

In eighteen-oh-four, the dawn broke bright,

The French were gone, their power slight.

Yet struggles brewed, the land was torn,

Two nations from one freedom born.

In northern realms, 'neath stars' embrace,

In eighteen-eleven, he found his place.

Henri the First, his kingdom wide,

With Citadelle, his strength and pride.

He sought to build, to educate,

To forge a realm both strong and great.

With palace grand and visions high,

He ruled with iron, reaching sky.

But harsh his methods, labor's pain,

Brought progress mixed with deep disdain.

As years went by, rebellion stirred,

In eighteen-twenty, his vision blurred.

In Sans-Souci's halls, his heart grew weak,

A stroke had left his spirit bleak.

Amid the strife, with rebels near,

He faced his fate, he quelled his fear.

In sorrow's grip, on October's day,

He took his life, in solemn sway.

Henri Christophe, both loved and feared,

A leader who dreamed, a king revered.

In Ayiti's tale, etched his legacy,

Carved in stone, in history's memory.

A monarch bold, with visions grand,

His story echoes across Ayiti's land.

Henri Christophe: The Defender of the Faith is a compelling narrative poem that delves into the complex and powerful legacy of Henri Christophe, one of Haiti's founding fathers. With vivid imagery and historical depth, the poem honors Christophe's heroic contributions to the Haitian Revolution, his bold rise as a leader, and his eventual reign as King Henri I. The poem captures his vision for a strong and prosperous

Haiti, symbolized by the grand Citadelle Laferrière, while also confronting the tension between his ambitious dreams and the hardships imposed by his rule. Through poignant verses, readers are invited to explore the resilience and contradictions of a man who helped shape Haiti's independence but ultimately faced internal rebellion and personal despair. Henri Christophe: The Defender of the Faith is a tribute to a leader whose aspirations echo through Haiti's history, offering a deep and thought-provoking exploration of leadership, legacy, and the costs of ambition.

Jacques Roumain: The Maestro of Haiti's Dawn

In Citadelle's realm, a child was born,
Destined to shape a nation's morn.
Jacques Roumain, with pen in hand,
Would cultivate his native land.

Through streets of poverty and strife,
He walked, absorbing Haitian life.
Each face a story, each voice a song,
Fueling words both brave and strong.

In Paris, where the storms of thought
Stirred minds to battles never fought,
Roumain absorbed the lightning's spark,
Dreaming of Haiti's bright rising arc.

Returning home, he met the snare,
The tyrant's wrath, the prison's glare.
Yet the iron bars could not confine
The burning truth of his design.

"Gouverneurs de la rosée," he wrote,
A masterpiece where hope would float.
Manuel's hands, Annaïse's tears,
A tale of love, of conquered fears.

Dry earth, once split by relentless rays,

Now flourishes, a verdant field ablaze.

United hearts made rivers freely flow,

A symbol of what the Haitian people sow.

His words outlived the prison's stone,

In every verse, a freedom grown.

His poetry, essays, prose—a rising tide,

Sweeping away the chains that bind.

Though his life was cut too soon,

His legacy remains under the moon.

In every Haitian's fervent heart,

Part of his dream finds a new start.

Let us honor this man of letters,

Who fought with words to break our fetters.

Jacques Roumain, whose words still dawn,

A light for those who journey on.

Jacques Roumain: The Maestro of Haiti's Dawn is a deeply evocative poem that celebrates the life and enduring legacy of one of Haiti's greatest literary figures. With vibrant imagery and historical resonance, the poem weaves Roumain's personal journey with the broader story of Haiti's struggle for identity and freedom. The piece honors his return to Haiti after studying in Paris, where his revolutionary ideas took root in the face of oppression. Central to the poem is Roumain's landmark work Gouverneurs de la rosée, which symbolizes the power of unity, love, and hope amidst hardship. Through poignant reflections on his time in prison and the enduring impact of his writing, the poem immortalizes Roumain's intellectual contributions as a beacon for future generations. His legacy, immortalized in the hearts and minds of the Haitian people, continues to inspire those who seek to break free from the chains of oppression and build a more hopeful future. Jacques Roumain: The Maestro of Haiti's Dawn is a powerful tribute to a visionary who used the written word as a tool for revolution and transformation.

Kompa's Melodic Heartbeat

In Haiti's heart, where oceans kiss the shore,

Kompa's rhythm, an ancient lore,

Whispers tales of a land so grand,

Where music weaves dreams in golden sand.

Beneath the palms, where breezes sigh,

Kompa's melody takes us high,

Through fields of sugarcane and rum,

A journey of beats, a kingdom come.

In Kompa's sway, history's embrace,

The struggle, the triumph, the timeless grace,

Melodies weave a tapestry strong,

Resilience in stories, a lifelong song.

From Cap-Haitien's streets to Jacmel's shores,

Kompa's pulse, a nation's core,

Guitar strings pluck memories untold,

Drums echo tales of legends old.

With every note, a dance of souls,

In Kompa's rhythms, hearts find their roles,

Love's dance in moonlit skies above,

A testament to Haiti's eternal love.

Oh, Kompa, in your melodies divine,

The spirit of a people, a sacred shrine,

In every beat, a history's scroll,

A nation's anthem, a timeless goal.

Let the music play on and on,

In Kompa's dance, our spirits are drawn,

A celebration of life's endless sway,

In Haiti's heart, Kompa holds its stay.

Kompa's Melodic Heartbeat is a captivating ode to Haiti's most beloved music genre, Kompa, that pulses through the nation's veins as both a cultural treasure and a powerful testament to the resilience and soul of its people. The poem paints a rich, lyrical portrait of Haiti, where Kompa's rhythm is inseparable from the land and its history. Each note, from the vibrant streets of Cap-Haitien to the laid-back shores of Jacmel, echoes the stories of love, revolution, and unity that have defined Haiti's journey. Through the poetic weave of guitar strings and drum beats, the music is elevated beyond sound to become a narrative of Haiti's enduring spirit, a symbol of resistance, celebration, and hope. Kompa is portrayed as a living, breathing force that binds generations, offering a profound connection to Haiti's heritage while inspiring the future. The poem calls for the eternal celebration of Kompa's melody, inviting the reader to partake in its dance and witness the unwavering heartbeat of a nation.

Port-au-Prince

In Port-au-Prince's vibrant, complex embrace,

A tapestry woven of beauty and disgrace.

Where streets are alive with colors, sounds, and tales,

Yet shadows linger, where hardship prevails.

Bustling markets, now echoes of the past,

Their vibrant spirit in memories cast.

Insecurities whisper in shadows deep,

Amidst the vibrancy, their secrets keep.

On Champ de Mars, where history reveals,

Laughter and protest, in tales that it seals.

Where vibrant art adorns the crumbling walls,

Echoes of past glories, amidst it all.

Carrefour's lively spirit, a bustling beat,

Where cultures blend in every street.

Petionville's elegance, hills adorned with grace,

A haven where dreams find a tranquil place.

Delmas' vibrant rhythm, a pulse of life,

Where dreams and aspirations blend in strife.

Port-au-Prince, a symphony of extremes,

Where dreams take flight in the sun's golden beams.

From the graceful hills to the urban sprawl,

Beauty and chaos, intertwined, enthrall.

Port-au-Prince, where the heart's beat is bold,

In its beauty and scars, yet stories untold.

Port-au-Prince is a striking tribute to the beating heart of Haiti, a city where beauty and adversity collide in a dance of history, culture, and struggle. The poem paints an evocative portrait of Haiti's capital, from its vibrant markets to its quiet, elegant hills, where the pulse of daily life reverberates through each corner of the city. Port-au-Prince emerges as a city of extremes: its bustling streets are alive with color and sound, while its scars reveal untold stories of hardship and resilience. Through neighborhoods like Champ de Mars, Carrefour, Petionville, and Delmas, the poem reflects the city's complex identity—where past glories and current challenges coalesce in a symphony of dreams, aspirations, and unspoken truths. The city's spirit, both bold and vulnerable, is celebrated as an enduring symbol of Haiti's unbreakable resolve. This poem invites readers to experience the emotional depth of Port-au-Prince, where beauty and chaos coexist, and where the dreams of its people soar above the shadows of the past.

Queen Anacaona of the Xaragua

In Xaragua's realm of lush green,

Ruled a queen of grace serene,

Anacaona, poetess bright,

Guiding her people with wisdom's light.

Her beauty shone like dawn's first ray,

In Taíno lands, where children play,

A leader fierce, yet heart so kind,

With every word, a love enshrined.

Beneath the Caribbean's azure skies,

She wove tales with soulful eyes,

Songs of peace and tales of lore,

Of ancient spirits, and much more.

Yet shadows loomed on distant shores,

As strangers knocked on island doors,

With promises and tongues of gold,

But hearts were dark and stories cold.

In friendship's name, she welcomed them,

With open arms, her diadem,

But treachery and greed conspired,

To bring her dreams to flames, they fired.

The feast was set, the halls were bright,

Yet betrayal struck that fateful night,

A massacre in blood was writ,

Innocence fell to power's fit.

Anacaona, captive queen,

In chains of fate, she stood serene,

Her spirit high, unbowed by fear,

In history's pages, crystal clear.

Symbol of strife, of peace and trust,

Justice, freedom, in shadows' gust,

Heart of Haiti, your heritage strong,

Anacaona, queen, in echoes long.

Queen Anacaona of the Xaragua is a poignant and timeless ode to the Taíno queen whose wisdom, beauty, and strength have transcended centuries. The poem captures the essence of Anacaona as a visionary leader, a poetess whose words and songs united her people under the Caribbean skies. Her grace and kindness stood in stark contrast to the dark forces that arrived on her shores—European colonizers whose promises of friendship masked the treachery that would lead to her people's downfall. The poem immortalizes her tragic betrayal and the massacre that followed, painting Anacaona as both a symbol of peace and a victim of colonial violence. Yet, despite her capture and the fall of her kingdom, Anacaona's unbroken spirit endures, standing as a beacon of resistance, justice, and strength. Her legacy is woven into Haiti's history, reminding us of the price of freedom and the resilience of those who fight for their land, their people, and their identity. The queen's name, forever etched in the echoes of time, continues to inspire as a symbol of enduring hope and the timeless struggle for liberation.

Soulful Rhythms of Cap-Haitian

In Cap-Haitian's lively streets,

Where laughter and music always meet,

People dance to life's rhythmic beat,

With history's echoes beneath their feet.

The Citadel stands, a silent guide,

Stories of courage it won't hide,

Whispers of freedom, far and wide,

In every stone, a hero's pride.

Market vendors' tales, vibrant and bright,

Share dreams that soar, taking flight,

In every greeting, a heartfelt invite,

To cherish moments, day or night.

Oh, Cap-Haitian, your pulse is strong,

In every voice, a timeless song,

A tapestry woven, rich and long,

Of resilience, where hearts belong.

From mountains' embrace to the sea's caress,

Cap-Haitian's spirit, a timeless dress,

In every face, a story to impress,

A city cherished, no words can express.

Soulful Rhythms of Cap-Haitian is an evocative celebration of one of Haiti's most vibrant and historically significant cities. The poem pulses with the rhythm of Cap-Haitian's lively streets, where music, laughter, and the spirit of the people intertwine, bringing the city to life. The iconic Citadel Laferrière, standing tall and proud, symbolizes the unwavering courage of Haiti's independence and the enduring pride of its people. From the bustling markets to the welcoming faces of its residents, Cap-Haitian embodies a sense of community and resilience, offering a haven where history and modernity dance in unison. The poem beautifully conveys the city's connection to the land, from its towering mountains to its sun-kissed shores, where every face tells a story of struggle, triumph, and enduring hope. Cap-Haitian is presented as a place where freedom, pride, and culture are celebrated, making it an eternal symbol of Haiti's strength and spirit.

Taste of Haiti

In Haiti's heart, where flavors dance,

A culinary gem, a cultural trance.

With spices bold, and heritage deep,

Its cuisine awakens senses from sleep.

From vibrant streets of Port-au-Prince,

To rural lands where traditions commence.

Each dish a story, each bite a song,

In Haiti's kitchens, you can't go wrong.

Griot, tender pork, marinated well,

With citrus and spices, a taste to tell.

Served with pikliz, a fiery delight,

Crunchy, tangy, with just the right bite.

Diri and djon djon, a rice so rare,

Black mushrooms lend their earthy flair.

A dish of love, a feast of pride,

In every grain, a nation's stride.

Lambi, the conch, from ocean's deep,

With garlic and herbs, memories to keep.

Tender and succulent, a true seaside treasure,

A Haitian dish that brings immense pleasure.

Soup Joumou, on New Year's Day,

A symbol of freedom, in a hearty array.

Pumpkin soup, rich, with a historical note,

In each spoonful, freedom's anthem floats.

Haitian food, a blend unique,

African roots, with a Creole tweak.

French, Spanish, Taíno, all combined,

In each meal, a journey defined.

What sets it apart, you might ask,

It's the love, the history, the culinary task.

Spices that sing, flavors that blend,

A Haitian meal is like a friend.

Warmth in each bite, soul in each dish,

Fulfilling more than just a taste wish.

In Haiti's cuisine, culture stands tall,

A flavorful embrace, inviting all.

When you savor that Haitian plate,

Remember the love, the history so great.

In every spice, a legacy's trace,

In every meal, Haiti's warm embrace.

Taste of Haiti is a flavorful tribute to the heart and soul
of Haitian cuisine, capturing the island's rich culinary tapestry

that is as diverse as its history. From the lively streets of Port-au-Prince to the intimate rural kitchens, the poem brings to life the vibrant and bold flavors that make Haitian food unforgettable. Signature dishes like griot, lambi, and soup joumou are immortalized in the poem, each one reflecting a cultural story—from the spicy kick of pikliz to the earthy depth of djon djon rice, every bite is a journey through Haiti's past and present. The poem celebrates the fusion of African, French, Spanish, and Taíno influences that create a truly unique and distinct Haitian flavor profile, one that invites all to partake in its warmth and joy. Taste of Haiti beautifully underscores how each meal is not just food but an expression of love, heritage, and a deep connection to the island's people. This culinary journey is an invitation to savor Haiti's legacy in every spice and seasoning, making it a perfect tribute to a nation defined by resilience and pride.

The Banner of Unity

In the land of mountains proud and free,

Where azure waves caress the shore,

A symbol rose for all to see,

A banner born from freedom's lore.

A tale of courage, brave and bold,

In Saint-Domingue's sunlit glade,

Where heroes' hearts and dreams unrolled,

The Haitian flag was proudly made.

Jean-Jacques Dessalines stood tall,

With Catherine Flon by his side,

They tore the tricolor's harsh thrall,

And stitched new hope with fervent pride.

With red and blue, they wove a dream,

Two bands of strength, of unity,

In freedom's light, their eyes did gleam,

A pledge to fight till liberty.

The flag they raised on that bright day,

A beacon for a nation's soul,

It marked the end of oppressive way,

And Haiti's quest for self-control.

Each year, in May, we celebrate,

With dances, songs, and voices clear,

Our flag's bright birth, our nation's fate,

The struggles past, we hold so dear.

With drums that echo through the night,

And flags that wave in joyful sway,

We honor those who dared to fight,

And cherish Haitian Flag Day.

Through storms and trials, it has flown,

Our emblem of a people's might,

A symbol of how far we've grown,

From darkest past to future bright.

Let us raise our voices high,

In unity, let's sing and cheer,

For Haiti's flag that waves in sky,

An emblem we love and revere.

The Banner of Unity is a stirring celebration of Haiti's enduring symbol of freedom—the Haitian flag. This poetic tribute honors the brave creation of the flag by Jean-Jacques Dessalines and Catherine Flon, marking the moment when the oppressive colonial tricolor was replaced by the red and blue that would come to represent Haiti's fight for independence and unity. The poem beautifully captures the powerful symbolism of the flag, highlighting its colors as a pledge to strength, unity, and the relentless pursuit of liberty. Each verse calls forth the pride and resilience of the Haitian people, invoking the historical significance of Haitian Flag Day and the deep reverence for the sacrifices made by those who fought for the nation's freedom. Through its rich imagery and stirring call to action, The Banner of Unity serves as both a reflection on Haiti's past and a hopeful anthem for its future, celebrating the enduring spirit of a nation that continues to rise.

Hayti: The Birth of a New Empire

In fields of cane, where freedom's seed

Lay dormant beneath oppression's creed,

A storm was brewing, fierce and bold—

Hayti's tale, waiting to be told.

"From Bwa Kayiman's sacred grove,

Where loa and liberty interwove,

I, Toussaint, lit the spark of change,

A flame no mortal could estrange."

The drums of war echoed through hills,

As slaves broke chains, defied king's wills.

In 1801, a constitution penned,

But France's grasp would not yet end.

"Our blood has watered freedom's tree,

Yet still we yearn to truly be

The masters of our destiny—

Oh Bondye, set your children free!"

Then rose Dessalines, vengeance incarnate,

In 1802, his fury innate.

With sword ablaze and eyes afire,

He vowed to build an empire.

The tricolor, once symbol of pain,

Now burned in pyres of disdain.

On New Year's Day, eighteen-oh-four,

A new flag rose on freedom's shore.

"No more to France!" the cry resounded,

In Gonaïves, our nation founded.

"We stand as men, no longer slaves!"

Hope blossomed from unmarked graves.

In Gonaïves, where history turned,

The Act was signed, oppression spurned.

A country built on broken chains,

Hayti emerged from centuries' pains.

The Constitution's pages bright,

In 1805, brought new light.

Each citizen a sovereign soul,

In Hayti's arms, the nation whole.

But power's thorns can prick the hand

That seeks to guide a newborn land.

October's leaves in 1806

Fell red with royal blood's cruel mix.

The land divided, North from South,

Twin nations from one freedom's mouth.

Christophe's kingdom, Pétion's domain,

Two visions for one proud terrain.

"Though leaders change and borders shift,

Our children's future is our gift.

In market, field, and mountain high,

Hayti's spirit will never die."

Years passed, and Boyer's steady hand

In 1820 reunites the land.

Yet challenges would ever loom

For this bright flower born of gloom.

From revolution's fiery test,

A beacon rose in the Caribbean's breast.

For Hayti stands, its flag unfurled,

Since 1804, inspiring the world.

Through storm and strife, through joy and pain,

Hayti's legacy shall ever remain:

A testament to human will,

Of liberty on freedom's hill.

Hayti: The Birth of a New Empire is a bold and evocative exploration of Haiti's revolutionary birth, blending the rich history of its struggle with the enduring spirit of freedom that defines the nation. The poem begins in the fields of oppression, where the flames of rebellion were kindled at Bwa Kayiman, igniting a fire that would burn away the chains of slavery. Toussaint Louverture's leadership laid the foundation for Haiti's independence, but it was Jean-Jacques Dessalines who transformed that dream into reality, declaring Haiti a free and sovereign nation on New Year's Day, 1804. The poem weaves through the tumultuous years of Haiti's early years, marked by division and struggle but underscored by the unbreakable will of its people. It reflects the courage of those who fought for liberty and the promise of a new empire, one built on the strength of the Haitian spirit. The poem ends with a reflection on Haiti's enduring legacy, emphasizing the country's role as a beacon of hope for freedom and a testament to the power of human resilience. Through vivid imagery and stirring language, Hayti: The Birth of a New Empire presents the heart of Haitian history as an anthem of pride, unity, and the unyielding pursuit of liberty.

The Flame of Freedom for Hayti

On tropic shores, where sugarcane stood tall,

A revolution's seed began to sprawl.

August twenty-two, seventeen ninety-one,

The drums of freedom had just begun.

In Bois Caïman, beneath a stormy sky,

Boukman's voice rang with a battle cry.

The Maroons blazed trails through mountains wide,

Their freedom the torch that turned the tide.

Then rose Toussaint, like a phoenix bright,

His mind a beacon in freedom's night.

From seventeen ninety-three, with tactical skill,

He bent great empires to his will.

With quill as mighty as his sword,

A constitution, his powerful word:

"No more shall slavery stain this land,

Free we stand, by our own command."

But Bonaparte schemed, and Toussaint fell,

Betrayed and imprisoned in a foreign cell.

His body captured, his dream lived on,

In hearts of those he had counted on.

Dessalines seized the torch of hope,

To scale sweet freedom's arduous slope.

January first, eighteen-oh-four,

Haiti emerged, freedom forevermore.

From blood-soaked fields to mountains high,

A nation's banner unfurled in the sky.

Toussaint's vision, by now fulfilled,

A testament to unyielding human will.

In annals of time, let it be known,

How slaves cast off oppression's throne.

Haiti's flame, eternally bright,

A beacon for all who seek freedom's light.

The Flame of Freedom for Hayti is a stirring narrative of Haiti's journey to independence, celebrating the bravery, resilience, and unity of its people. The poem vividly portrays key events, beginning with the August 1791 uprising at Bois Caïman, led by Boukman, whose rallying cry ignited a revolution. It honors the leadership of Toussaint Louverture, a master tactician and visionary, who embodied the fight for freedom and equality, drafting a constitution that declared the end of slavery. Despite his betrayal and death, the poem reflects on how his spirit endured, inspiring Jean-Jacques Dessalines to complete the mission. Haiti's declaration of independence on January 1, 1804, marked the dawn of a free nation, the first black republic, and a testament to the unyielding will of its people.

Through rich imagery and evocative language, the poem captures the sacrifice and triumph of the Haitian Revolution, symbolizing a flame of freedom that continues to burn brightly. It positions Haiti not only as a nation but as a global symbol of liberation and resilience. This work is both an homage to Haiti's heroes and an inspiration for all who seek justice and self-determination.

The Unknown Maroon: The Trailblazers of Rebellion

In shadows deep where whispers hide,

The Unknown Maroon walks with pride.

Through forests dense, their spirit roams,

A rebel's heart, a warrior's home.

Chains they broke, to freedom's call,

They rose, they fought, and stood tall.

In hidden realms of tangled green,

Their remnant, a timeless scene.

No names are etched on history's page,

Yet in their deeds, a mighty rage.

Against oppression's cruel embrace,

They carved a path, a sacred space.

With every step, a silent vow,

To live unchained, to never bow.

Their courage blooms in nature's heart,

A flame of hope, a rebel's art.

Sing their song, the Unknown Maroon,

A tale of freedom, to the moon.

In every jungle, their echoes ring,

A testament to strength they bring.

In silent groves, their story thrives,

An anthem sung by untamed lives.

They dance with shadows, wild and free,

The Unknown Maroon, immortal legacy.

The Unknown Maroon: The Trailblazers of Rebellion is a poetic homage to the unsung heroes of freedom—the Maroons. Through evocative imagery and stirring verses, it celebrates their indomitable spirit, their defiance against oppression, and their enduring legacy etched in the untamed landscapes they once called home. This poem weaves a powerful narrative of resilience, highlighting the Maroons' silent yet profound contribution to the fight for liberty. Their legacy, immortalized in nature's whispers and the echoes of rebellion, inspires a timeless anthem of courage and unyielding strength.

Echoes of Vertières

Atop the hills, where the cannons once roared,
The Battle of Vertières, a saga adored.
Fought with passion, against the chains that bind,
In the hearts of the Haitians, liberty enshrined.

Dessalines, the lion, with a vision so clear,
Leading the charge, banishing doubt and fear.
Capois, a warrior, with a dream so divine,
To break the shackles, let freedom shine.

Toussaint, a phoenix risen from the slave's lament,
His spirit ablaze, with a fervor unspent.
A beacon of hope, amid the chaos and despair,
In the hallowed struggle, a legend to declare.

Henri Christophe, a visionary, builder of dreams,
Amidst the conflict and chaos, his legacy gleams.
Cécile Fatiman, priestess of vodou's embrace,
Her prayers echoed in the drumbeats of grace.

A mystic force, in the revolution's trance,
Guiding the rebels in their daring dance.
Women warriors, with courage untamed,
Names etched in history, valor proclaimed.

Haiti's sons and daughters, united they stood,

In the face of oppression, they withstood.

Vertières, a testament, etched in the earth,

Of a people's resilience, of freedom's birth.

Echoes of Vertières, is a lyrical tribute to Haiti's pivotal triumph in the Battle of Vertières, where courage and unity forged the first independent Black republic. The poem vividly captures the heroism of iconic figures like Dessalines, Toussaint, Capois, Henri Christophe, and Cécile Fatiman, alongside the unnamed warriors whose sacrifices illuminated Haiti's path to freedom. Interwoven with themes of resilience and mystic strength, it honors the revolutionaries' defiance against oppression and the collective spirit that birthed a legacy of liberation.

The Pearl of the Islands

Hayti, the Pearl of islands, so rare,

A gem in the Caribbean, beyond compare,

In your vibrant heart, your beauty unfurls,

A treasure of nature, a haven of pearls.

Land of mountains, rising to the sky,

Majestic peaks where dreams dare to fly,

Their grandeur and might, a sight to behold,

In their shadow, your story is told.

First Black Republic, a historic stand,

Colonial chains, you broke free from the land,

Through rebellions, you fought for the light,

Emerging as a symbol, shining so bright.

Descendants of Dahomey, your bloodline strong,

A connection to roots, where you truly belong,

Inheritors of courage, resilience, and pride,

Your ancestors' spirits, forever by your side.

Hayti, your people, a force to reckon,

With a history so rich, their heritage beckon,

In drumbeats and hums, their legacy's tune,

Resonates forever, beneath the Caribbean moon.

The Pearl of Islands is a poetic celebration of Haiti's unparalleled beauty, resilience, and historical significance. With vivid imagery, the poem portrays Haiti as a radiant gem of the Caribbean, its majestic mountains and storied past standing as testaments to its enduring spirit. From the triumph of becoming the first Black republic to the indomitable courage of its descendants, the verses honor the nation's vibrant culture, deep-rooted heritage, and connection to its African ancestry.

To the Women of Haiti

In Haiti's vibrant, sun-kissed land,

Where a remarkable history unfurls,

As resilient as the ever-shifting sand,

Haitian women stand, like precious pearls.

With skin kissed by the Caribbean sun,

They bear the weight of history's page,

Through struggles and battles, they've won,

Writing their own story on a different stage.

In their eyes, a timeless splendor,

Reflects the strength of their ancestry,

Their beauty, a lasting narrative to render,

A legacy of resilience and tenacity.

Their laughter, a melody, pure and sweet,

Echoes through mountains and boundless sea,

In hardship, their spirit, with strength complete,

Forever untamed and unbridled, wild and free.

They are the heartbeat of this nation,

An embodiment of life's resplendence,

Their courage, a source of inspiration,

Holding tight to their enduring presence.

To the Women of Haiti is a heartfelt ode to the enduring strength, beauty, and resilience of Haitian women. Through lush imagery and evocative verses, the poem honors their role as the pillars of a nation's legacy. It celebrates their courage in adversity, their unbreakable spirit, and their timeless connection to Haiti's vibrant culture and history. From their laughter echoing through the land to their unyielding determination, Haitian women are portrayed as the soul of their nation—a source of life, hope, and inspiration.

Chapter Five

The Poetic Odyssey of the Power Within

Life is an epic journey, a masterpiece painted with the vivid hues of triumph and trial, each stroke telling a story of resilience. In this chapter, The Poetic Odyssey of the Power Within, we embark on a transformative exploration of the human spirit's extraordinary capacity to endure, evolve, and rise. Through the timeless lens of poetry, we delve into the essence of resilience—a force that defines our identities, fuels our aspirations, and lights the way through life's darkest moments.

Every individual's story is a symphony of struggles and victories, resonating with universal chords of perseverance. Whether confronting personal heartbreak, societal injustice, or the relentless pressure of expectation, the journey toward resilience is one we all share. It is a path marked by uncertainty and challenge, yet within its trials lies the power to bloom anew—to transform pain into purpose, vulnerability into strength, and despair into hope.

This chapter invites you to traverse poetic landscapes that echo the trials and triumphs of countless souls. Each verse reveals a story of courage born from hardship, a reflection of the indomitable spirit that binds humanity together. These poems do not merely narrate resilience—they embody it, offering a mirror to your own battles and victories. They remind us that resilience thrives not in the absence of adversity but in its very presence, blossoming like wildflowers through the cracks of life's hardest terrains.

Resilience is not a solitary force; it is cultivated in the company of others. The love of family, the support of friends, and the strength of community act as pillars that sustain us through life's storms. This chapter celebrates these connections, showing how the bonds we form empower us to face even the fiercest challenges. Together, we find the courage to persist, to heal, and to grow stronger.

As you turn the pages of this poetic odyssey, reflect on your own journey. Consider the moments when you stood at the crossroads of despair and chose to rise, the lessons etched in scars that now gleam with wisdom, and the beauty you discovered in the struggle. Let these verses remind you of the strength that lies within, a force as boundless as the human spirit itself.

May The Poetic Odyssey of the Power Within inspire you to embrace your journey with newfound courage. Let it be a testament to the shared resilience that unites us—a timeless anthem of hope, determination, and the enduring light that guides us all forward. Together, let us honor the power within us, celebrating the triumph of the human spirit in the face of life's greatest trials.

A Journey Through Truth and Understanding

In the journey's depths, truths unfurl,

Where paths entwine, and stories swirl.

You think you know, but yet you find,

The layers of a soul, in every kind.

Traveling together, roads untold,

Reveals the facets, both new and old.

In unfamiliar lands, hearts laid bare,

Moments shared, beyond compare.

Money's dance, a tangled thread,

Where trust is tested, words unsaid.

Navigating currencies, desires clash,

Unveiling truths, in the coin's harsh flash.

Anger's fire, a tempest's roar,

Tests the bonds, like never before.

Emotions raw, tempers ignite,

In the heat of passion, truth takes flight.

Living side by side, day by day,

Reveals the hues, in every way.

From morning light to midnight's shade,

The real self emerges, unafraid.

One truly knows another soul,

When life's varied chapters unroll.

Amidst travels, wealth, and fury's trace,

Love and grace reveal truth's face.

A Journey Through Truth and Understanding is a poetic exploration of the multifaceted nature of human relationships, revealed through shared experiences, challenges, and emotions. The poem journeys through themes of trust, conflict, and vulnerability, uncovering the raw truths that emerge when lives intertwine deeply. From the complexities of financial tensions to the fiery trials of anger, it portrays the resilience of bonds tested by life's pressures.

Ultimately, the poem celebrates the beauty of self-discovery and mutual understanding that arises from living, loving, and journeying together. It highlights how true connection is forged not in perfection but in navigating the imperfect, revealing the heart's authentic depths.

A Poetic Journey Through Depression

In the depths where shadows dwell,

A silent storm, a whispered hell.

Dark tendrils coil, emotions swell,

In the heart's abyss, thoughts rebel.

The weight of sorrow, a heavy chain,

Binding the soul in endless pain.

A shattered mirror, reflections wane,

Lost in the maze of a troubled brain.

Whispers of doubt, a haunting choir,

In the quietude of midnight's dire.

Aching hearts, consumed by fire,

Yearning for hope, to lift them higher.

Amidst the darkness, a flicker of light,

Strength, pushing through the night.

Courage rises, in the soul's delight,

To fight the shadows, reclaim the sight.

In the journey of the heart's despair,

There's resilience found, beyond compare.

Through tears and fears, we learn to bear,

And find the dawn, in the depths of care.

Oh! hold on tight, when darkness looms,

For even in silence, hope still blooms.

Heart's endurance, a melody that resumes,

Symphony of courage, breaking gloom's tombs.

A Poetic Journey Through Depression is a profound and empathetic exploration of the silent struggles faced in the depths of despair. Through vivid imagery and lyrical rhythm, the poem captures the overwhelming weight of sorrow, the haunting whispers of doubt, and the consuming darkness of depression. Yet, within this bleak landscape, it offers a beacon of hope—a testament to the strength of the human spirit, the courage to confront inner shadows, and the resilience to rise from despair.

This poignant piece not only reflects the raw emotions of those battling depression but also serves as a reminder of the transformative power of endurance and hope. It speaks to the universal experience of struggle and the shared journey toward healing and light.

A Poetic Voyage Beyond Heartache

In the silence of a shattered heart,

Where echoes of love once played their part,

Comes the journey of healing and growth,

Navigating life's tumultuous oath.

Through the tears that blur the path,

We find strength to rise from aftermath,

A phoenix soaring from the ashes of pain,

Embracing the sunshine after the rain.

The road ahead may seem unclear,

Yet each step brings us near,

To rediscovering who we are meant to be,

In the vast expanse of possibility.

We learn to cherish solitude's embrace,

Embracing our flaws with grace,

For in the depths of self-reflection,

We find the power of resurrection.

Love may have faltered and dreams may fade,

But resilience and courage never evade,

As we rebuild from broken pieces anew,

Embracing life's beauty, bold and true.

Let the past be a stepping stone,

To a future where we stand alone,

Stronger, wiser, and unafraid,

A poetic voyage, undeterred and unswayed.

A Poetic Voyage Beyond Heartache is a moving exploration of the journey to rediscover oneself after the devastation of lost love. Through evocative imagery and uplifting verses, the poem charts a path from the depths of sorrow to the heights of renewal. It reflects on the pain of heartbreak, the strength found in solitude, and the power of resilience to transform loss into a stepping stone for growth.

With its themes of healing, self-reflection, and inner strength, the poem inspires readers to embrace life's challenges as opportunities for rebirth. It reminds us that even in heartache, there is beauty to be found and a brighter future to create.

Embracing True Self

In the mirror's gaze, I find my light,
A beacon glowing through the night.
With every flaw and every scar,
I stand tall, a radiant star.

Embracing curves, the lines that trace,
The journey etched upon my face.
Strength and grace in every stride,
A testament to the love inside.

No longer bound by doubts and fears,
I wipe away those fallen tears.
In self-love's warm and tender hold,
I shine with courage, pure and bold.

Empowered heart, a spirit free,
Unchained by what the world might see.
I dance to rhythms of my soul,
In every beat, I feel whole.

To those who journey, seek, and strive,
Remember you are truly alive.
In love's embrace, let self-worth rise,
For in your eyes, your beauty lies.

Embracing True Self is a powerful celebration of self-love, confidence, and the transformative journey toward self-acceptance. Through lyrical beauty, the poem explores the strength found in embracing one's imperfections and the radiant power that emerges when we free ourselves from fear and doubt. It paints a portrait of a spirit that rises above societal expectations, dancing to its own rhythm, and finding beauty in every scar and flaw.

This poem serves as an anthem for personal empowerment, encouraging readers to honor their true selves and recognize the inherent beauty and strength they carry within.

Essence of Simplicity

In simple things, peace we find,

In gentle hearts, our worries unwind.

To love with ease, to live with grace,

Is a joy fleeting time cannot erase.

In tranquil hours, truth reveals,

The humble power that life conceals.

A dew-kissed morning, a twilight glow,

Life's true treasures we come to know.

Through nature's verdant sweep,

A silent promise, secrets we keep.

In every leaf and petal's hue,

The world's beauty shines anew.

No need for splendor, nor for gold,

In whispered stories, love is told.

A cup of tea, a heartfelt tune,

In these, our humble souls commune.

The laughters shared, tears we dry,

Beneath the vast, unending sky.

Find joy in quiet, still repose,

Where peace in simplicity grows.

A breath of air, a silent prayer,

Contentment found in moments rare.

For in the end, it's crystal clear,

Simplicity holds what we hold dear.

In fleeting clouds and morning's light,

In the serene stillness of the night,

Simplicity speaks in a voice so true,

A gentle reminder of what we pursue.

That life's most precious, enduring gift,

Is found in the moments we uplift.

In loving simply, and in living free,

We find the essence of simplicity.

Essence of Simplicity is a serene and introspective celebration of life's most meaningful treasures found in the quiet, unassuming moments. The poem explores the profound peace and contentment that arises when we embrace simplicity—whether in nature, relationships, or the small joys of daily life. Through vivid imagery, it invites readers to find beauty in the ordinary and reminds them that true wealth lies in the humblest of experiences: a shared laugh, a moment of stillness, or the peaceful breath of dawn.

The poem serves as a gentle yet powerful reminder that in a world often driven by complexity and materialism, simplicity is the path to true fulfillment and joy.

I Am the Goat

In life's vast range, a journey unfolds,

A tale of peaks, with stories untold.

With hooves that echo on paths unknown,

I am the goat, strength I've sown.

On craggy slopes where challenges rise,

I find my footing, gaze to the skies.

A crown of courage, steadfast and bold,

With every daring step, a story is told.

Through misty valleys and storms that break,

I am the goat, unshaken, awake.

A dance with trials, a ballet of strife,

Navigating cliffs of this mountainous life.

Majestic in struggle, resilient in grace,

I climb towards dreams in a determined chase.

With every ascent, a lesson is gleaned,

In rugged terrain, my spirit is seen.

In meadows of joy, where dreams interweave,

I find solace, and in myself, believe.

For in this journey, both fierce and remote,

Resilient and poised, I am the goat.

I am the Goat is an empowering ode to resilience, strength, and unwavering determination. The poem portrays the speaker as the metaphorical goat, navigating life's challenges with grace, courage, and a steadfast spirit. With each mountain climbed and each trial faced, the poem celebrates the pursuit of dreams, the lessons learned through struggle, and the triumph of the human spirit over adversity.

Through vivid imagery and rhythmic flow, the poem paints a powerful picture of tenacity, highlighting how, like the goat, one can conquer obstacles, find beauty in resilience, and emerge victorious.

Inward Journey to Self-Love

In the quiet night, as the mind drifts away,

A soul searches, lost in this intricate fray.

The world outside gleams, yet the heart is in a phase,

Of no calm, no peace, just a turbulent craze.

Deep within, a battle rages, unseen but real,

Between self-love and wounds that never heal.

Whispers of doubt, fears that silently accuse,

Casting shadows where light should ideally infuse.

But amidst this chaos, a voice breaks through,

Singing of worth, of renewed strength too.

It whispers the key, to understand within,

To embrace our flaws with kindness, a gentle spin.

Oh, how crucial it is, this love for oneself,

Like a treasure found on a forgotten shelf.

For how can we give if we're empty, bereft?

To love others wholly, our own love must be deft.

Let's raise our glasses to self-care and healing,

To wounds that mend despite life's painful feeling.

For in loving ourselves, we find a serene place,

A life lived authentically, with love as our base.

Inward Journey to Self-Love is a heartfelt exploration of the internal struggle to embrace self-love and healing. The poem delves into the chaos of self-doubt, fear, and unhealed wounds, juxtaposed with the quiet, powerful voice of self-empowerment and worth. It reminds us that the path to loving others starts with the crucial task of loving oneself. Through vivid metaphors and soothing rhythm, the poem emphasizes the importance of self-care, self-compassion, and the transformative power of inner peace.

The message of the poem is both personal and universal, offering readers an invitation to pause, reflect, and find healing through self-acceptance.

The Biggest Failure in Life

The biggest failure in life is when
Dreams wither in the mind,
When doubts and fears, like shadows, cast
Your courage far behind.

It's not the falls that etch the pain
Or scars upon your soul,
But when you trade the dawn's embrace
For night's unyielding toll.

When faith in self dissolves to dust,
And hope's a distant star,
When passion's flame is dimmed by time,
You lose sight of who you are.

True failure lives in letting go,
In succumbing to despair,
In silencing the voice within
That whispers you still care.

Rise anew, despite the path
That winds through dark and light,
For in your heart, resilience burns,
A beacon in the night.

The biggest failure in life is when

You let your spirit die,

Yet triumph blooms in every step

That dares to reach the sky.

The Biggest Failure in Life is a powerful meditation on resilience, self-doubt, and the triumph of perseverance. The poem explores the true essence of failure—not in the missteps or hardships we face, but in the moments when we let fear, self-doubt, and despair extinguish our dreams. Through poignant imagery and a stirring call to rise again, the poem encourages readers to embrace their inner strength, to reignite their passions, and to never lose sight of the light within, no matter how dark the path may seem.

The poem inspires hope and determination, offering a profound reminder that failure is not falling, but giving up on the pursuit of what truly matters. It speaks directly to the universal experience of overcoming personal struggles and embracing the resilience to keep moving forward.

Rise of the Phoenix

In the ashes of yesterday's sorrow,

A spark of hope ignites tomorrow.

From the ruins of dreams once shattered,

A new dawn rises, undeterred and unfettered.

Through trials faced and battles fought,

Strength is born, lessons taught.

In the heart of darkness, a flame burns bright,

Guiding the way, a beacon of light.

We are the phoenix, rising anew,

From the flames, our spirit grew.

In every fall, there's a hidden grace,

A chance to rebuild, to find our place.

With every tear and every scar,

We shine brighter, like a distant star.

In unity and love, we find our way,

Together, we conquer, come what may.

So, let us rise, let our voices sing,

Of hope, resilience, and everything.

For in the ashes, we'll always find,

The strength to soar, the will to climb.

Rise of the Phoenix is a stirring anthem of renewal, resilience, and the transformative power of hope. The poem beautifully symbolizes the human spirit as a phoenix, rising from the ashes of despair and adversity. With each trial and setback, the poem reminds us that there is strength in struggle, grace in falling, and always an opportunity for rebirth. It speaks to the universal experience of overcoming hardship, embracing growth, and finding new purpose through pain.

The poem is a call to action, urging readers to rise above their challenges, together, and to harness the inner strength that lives within them. Through vivid imagery and empowering language, it evokes the image of a collective journey toward healing, making it both uplifting and motivating.

Sacred Evolution

Vibrations flow through space and time,
Our feelings draw what's yours and mine.
When thoughts turn real, we're bound to act,
Through sacred fails, we stay intact.

Each stumble teaches what we need,
From "no" to "yes" - divine seeds lead.
Breathe deep and calm when storms attack,
The universe has got your back.

Life stretches long, we press ahead,
New wisdom blooms from tears we've shed.
No room for fear when spirit's high,
The divine summit calls those who try.

Don't wait for gifts that others bring,
Grow gardens where your soul can sing.
Your moment's coming, trust this grace,
In cosmic time, you'll find your place.

Judge all the same - both friend and blood,
See clear through karma's storm and flood.
Fear not the fall, take faith's pure leap,
For stagnant dreams are death's slow creep.

Each soul has purpose, blessed and true,

A fish can't climb, but knows what's due.

So, lift your gaze to what could be,

And shape the self God meant to free.

Sacred Evolution explores the deep spiritual connection between personal growth, the universe, and divine timing. Through poetic imagery and profound wisdom, the poem reflects on the journey of self-discovery, resilience, and the sacred path of evolution. It encourages embracing life's challenges as opportunities for growth and wisdom, trusting that the universe has a plan for each individual. The poem calls readers to rise above fear, to cultivate their inner gardens, and to understand that every step, stumble, and triumph is a part of a divine cosmic order.

The poem also touches on the importance of self-empowerment, urging individuals to honor their unique purpose and take action toward fulfilling their potential. The message is one of patience, faith, and alignment with the universe, resonating deeply with those who seek peace, understanding, and personal evolution.

Sanctuary of Fractured Minds

In hushed corridors where echoes sleep,
And phantom guardians vigil keep,
A fortress stands, a gossamer veil,
For psyches scarred by unseen gale.

These walls, mute witnesses to silent screams,
Cradle the fragments of shattered dreams.
Each teardrop, each thought—a broken shard,
Meets tender balm, by empathy starred.

While outside, the world may avert its gaze,
Here, darkness dances with hope's soft rays.
In sterile rooms, resilience takes root,
Where withered spirits yield hard-won fruit.

For those adrift in mind's tempestuous sea,
These bounds are not captivity, but key.
You're heard in whispers, seen through misted eyes,
A beacon piercing through delusion's guise.

Let society peer through our fractured lens,
And glimpse the strength that adversity lends.
No stigma clings, no judgment mars this space,
Where broken souls find healing's warm embrace.

In every labored breath, each muffled cry,
Determination murmurs, "Dare to fly."
For in this crucible of pain and grace,
New dawns are forged in time's relentless race.

Through corridors of healing, softly tread,
Where ghosts of former selves are gently shed.
In this asylum—both refuge and stage—
The valiant pen their lives' most crucial page.

Sanctuary of Fractured Minds delves into the complex and often hidden experience of mental health, portraying a space where those who suffer can find healing and understanding. The poem introduces a metaphorical sanctuary where fragmented minds are not only welcomed but nurtured. The "silent screams" and "shattered dreams" are given room for healing, as empathy and resilience gently mend what is broken. The imagery of dark corridors where "darkness dances with hope's soft rays" speaks to the delicate balance between despair and the promise of recovery.

This powerful piece dismantles the stigma surrounding mental health, inviting society to see the strength within those often marginalized. The walls of the sanctuary do not hold captives; rather, they offer a key to freedom, emphasizing the importance of self-compassion, inner strength, and community support in the healing process. The phrase "Where broken souls find healing's warm embrace" conveys a message of hope and renewal, reminding readers that pain can be transformative, and from it, new beginnings emerge.

Sitting with My Thoughts

Amidst the whispers of gentle breeze,

A haven found in moments alone,

From noises that seek to displease,

In quietude, my peace is grown.

No clamor of voices, no chaotic sound,

Just the melody of my own heartbeat,

In this quiet space, I am unbound,

From the worries that often compete.

No drama unfolds, no conflicts arise,

Only serenity, like a soothing stream,

Beneath the vast and starlit skies,

A tranquil dream, a peaceful scheme.

No judgments cast, no pretense to bear,

Authenticity shines, pure and true,

In contemplation, I'm free to share,

The depths of my soul, without ado.

Cherishing moments, precious and rare,

Away from tumult, far from the crowd,

In the intimacy of solace and care,

With my thoughts, peaceful and proud.

Sitting with My Thoughts delves into the complex and often hidden experience of mental health, portraying a space where those who suffer can find healing and understanding. The poem introduces a metaphorical sanctuary where fragmented minds are not only welcomed but nurtured. The "silent screams" and "shattered dreams" are given room for healing, as empathy and resilience gently mend what is broken. The imagery of dark corridors where "darkness dances with hope's soft rays" speaks to the delicate balance between despair and the promise of recovery.

This powerful piece dismantles the stigma surrounding mental health, inviting society to see the strength within those often marginalized. The walls of the sanctuary do not hold captives; rather, they offer a key to freedom, emphasizing the importance of self-compassion, inner strength, and community support in the healing process. The phrase "Where broken souls find healing's warm embrace" conveys a message of hope and renewal, reminding readers that pain can be transformative, and from it, new beginnings emerge.

The Journey Within

In the hum of life's rhythm, we sway to unseen tunes,

Emotions, like magnets, pull us through highs and swoons.

Thoughts take shape, urging us to leap into the fray,

Failures don't deter, they guide, making us stronger each day.

Breathe in deep, as stress knocks at your door,

Recall conquered mountains, they've paved your way for more.

Life's a novel, chapters unfold, stories to be read,

Triumphs and trials, each a thread in the tapestry ahead.

Mistakes are but footprints on the sands we traverse,

A rebirth granted, a second chance, a blessing we immerse.

No fear resides within, only a burning desire,

To climb the peaks where dreams aspire.

The road less traveled is lonely, but the view is sweet,

Plant your own roses, nurture dreams at your feet.

In the court of judgment, treat kin and friend alike,

Blood runs deep, but love's bond is the true light.

Fear not the stumble, for trying is victory,

Procrastination, a silent waltz, a fading melody.

Each life, a purpose unfolding, unique as a tree,

Open your eyes, and see the human you aspire to be.

The Journey Within is a powerful and inspirational reflection on life's obstacles and triumphs. It invites readers to embrace personal growth through resilience, viewing failures and mistakes as opportunities for strength and self-discovery. With its focus on inner peace, the nurturing of dreams, and the importance of love and human connection, this poem serves as a reminder that the road to success is uniquely our own, full of challenges that shape us into the people we aspire to be. It resonates with anyone who seeks motivation, healing, and the courage to rise above life's trials.

The Light of Innate Knowing

In the dawn's first light, I awoke,

Not to whispers of belief, but to knowing,

For within my soul, bespoke,

Truth was an eternal river, flowing.

Belief, a shadow cast by doubt,

A fragile thread of whispered pleas,

But in my heart, there's no devout,

For uncertainty to seize.

Born with eyes that pierce the veil,

Seeing truths that others seek,

In every tale, in every trail,

My understanding, clear and sleek.

No need for faith to guide my way,

For knowledge is my steadfast guide,

With clarity, both night and day,

My inner light, a constant tide.

Belief may falter, ebb, and fade,

A fleeting grasp at shadows cast,

But knowledge, bold and unafraid,

Is the seed within me, vast.

Here I stand, in firm embrace,

Of truths that in my spirit lie,

A journey led by knowledge's grace,

Beneath an endless, boundless sky.

Through the winds of doubt and fear,

My path remains both true and bright,

For in my soul, it's crystal clear,

Knowledge is my guiding light.

The Light of Innate Knowing presents a profound meditation on the unwavering power of self-knowledge. The poem speaks to those who have experienced the shift from fragile belief to a deep, internal certainty. It highlights the transformative strength of knowing one's truth, unaffected by doubt or fleeting faith. With its timeless message of clarity and confidence, this poem resonates with anyone seeking a path illuminated by inner wisdom, encouraging the embrace of knowledge as both a guiding force and a source of enduring peace.

A Symphony of Wisdom

In the twilight of the sun, a youth's heart spoke,

To the Poet, wise and old, these words awoke:

Tell me, Psalmist of the years, your sacred song,

The secrets of life's tapestry, woven strong.

In the garden of my dreams, blooms ambition bright,

A symphony of hopes, a radiant light.

Speak to me of paths, where wisdom gently weaves,

Through valleys deep, and mountains crowned with leaves.

Oh, Sage, unlock the door to knowledge vast,

Reveal the truths of futures, present, and past.

What melodies are hidden in the quiet stream,

What whispers of the moon, in the poet's dream?

Guide me, as the stars guide sailors on the sea,

Illuminate the shadows, set my spirit free.

Yet, heed, for youth's fire burns with fervent flame,

Eager, I crave, to inscribe my name.

In the scrolls of time, let my story be told,

A sonnet penned in letters of shimmering gold.

The Psalmist, with eyes that held the universe's gaze,

Spoke with kindness, through the corridors of days:

Youthful seeker, brimming with life's sweet song,

In the tapestry of time, you too belong.

The garden of dreams, where aspirations bloom,

Is tended by both sunlight and shadow's gloom.

Paths of wisdom wind through the heart's terrain,

Each step a lesson, each trial a gain.

The symphony of hopes, let its music play,

But learn the cadence of both night and day.

The door to knowledge swings wide, my friend,

Yet in the journey, let patience attend.

The stream of life whispers tales untold,

Listen with a heart, both tender and bold.

Stars may guide, but your compass lies within,

Navigate with courage, let your journey begin.

And as for fire, let it warm, not consume,

Inscribe your name with grace, not just with plume.

For in the scrolls of time, where stories unfold,

May your sonnet be written in letters of gold.

And so, the youth embarked on life's grand quest,

A symphony of dreams, with wisdom as his guest.

A Symphony of Wisdom beautifully captures the timeless
exchange between youthful ambition and seasoned wisdom.

Through a dialogue between a curious youth and a wise poet, the poem explores the balance between dreams and reality, ambition and patience, and the pursuit of knowledge. It resonates with readers at all stages of life, reminding them that the path to success is shaped by both triumphs and challenges. With its rich imagery and profound messages, this poem inspires a journey of self-discovery, urging readers to approach their dreams with both boldness and wisdom, and to leave a lasting, graceful mark on the world.

The Battle of Life

In the theater of life, a war unfolds,

A battle fought by young and growing souls.

With courage, we march through the darkest night,

Seeking meaning, searching for the light.

Through trials and tribulations, we persist,

And in our hearts, a flicker of hope exists.

For in the crucible of struggle, we find,

The purpose that unites all of humankind.

In trenches dug by time, we take our stand,

United by the ties of fate and hand in hand.

Though war may rage within, and battles scar,

We rise above, reaching for that distant star.

In the chaos of existence, we seek the truth,

A common thread that binds our restless youth.

In love and loss, in joy and deep despair,

Life's battles forge the souls we are to bear.

So, let us soldier on, and not relent,

In life's vast war, let love and kindness vent.

The general purpose of our mortal strife,

Is to embrace the beauty of this life.

The Battle of Life is a powerful metaphor for the universal struggle that defines the human experience. Through its vivid imagery of war and resilience, the poem speaks to the trials and triumphs that shape individuals as they seek meaning and purpose. It resonates with readers facing their own challenges, offering hope that love, kindness, and perseverance will guide them through life's battles. With its compelling message of unity and the transformative power of struggle, this poem inspires readers to embrace life's chaos with strength and grace, finding beauty in every fight for purpose.

Closing Reflections

As we reach the final pages of My Poetic Odyssey, we find ourselves immersed in a rich tapestry of five essential themes: love, identity, nature, Haiti, and resilience. Each chapter has been a gateway, inviting us to explore universal truths and reflect on our shared human experiences, weaving together connections that transcend the boundaries of time and place.

Love emerges as the unyielding force that anchors us all. Through tender verses and impassioned declarations, this chapter explored love in its infinite forms—romantic, platonic, and self-love. It is the thread that binds us, revealing the transformative power of vulnerability, intimacy, and compassion. These poems remind us that love is not merely an emotion but a practice, a daily choice that deepens our connections and enriches our lives.

Identity calls us to the core of who we are, celebrating the intricate mosaic of our individual and collective stories. Through poetry, we have unraveled the ways our experiences, culture, and memories shape us. This chapter embraced the fluidity of identity, highlighting how it evolves as we grow, love, and learn. It is a testament to the beauty of self-discovery and the interconnectedness of our personal narratives.

Nature provides both solace and revelation, its rhythms echoing the cycles of our own lives. The poems in this chapter transport us to vibrant landscapes and quiet corners, where the lessons of patience, renewal, and balance are ever-present. Nature becomes not only a backdrop but a mirror, reflecting the profound truths of existence and reminding us to find harmony in the chaos.

Our journey to *Haiti* illuminated the richness of a culture and history that pulses with resilience and vibrancy. Through these verses, we celebrated the enduring spirit of a nation shaped by struggle and triumph. The poetry honored Haiti's beauty, strength, and cultural legacy, encouraging a deeper understanding of its soul. These stories are both a tribute to the past and a vision for a brighter, unified future.

Finally, *resilience* stands as the heartbeat of this collection—a tribute to the strength that arises from adversity. Life's challenges test us, but they also forge the unyielding spirit within. The poems in this chapter resonate with hope and determination, offering a reminder that even in our darkest moments, we possess the power to rise, rebuild, and thrive.

As you close this book, I invite you to carry these themes into your own life. Embrace love with an open heart, honor the essence of your identity, draw strength from the beauty of nature, celebrate the richness of culture, and nurture resilience in the face of life's challenges. Your personal odyssey is waiting—filled with untold stories, meaningful connections, and infinite possibilities.

Thank you for embarking on this journey with me. May these verses inspire you to explore your own poetic path, finding beauty, strength, and wonder in every chapter of your life.

Acknowledgments

As I reflect on the journey of creating My Poetic
Odyssey, my heart overflows with gratitude for the love and
encouragement that have carried me through this creative
endeavor. This book is not merely a collection of poems; it is
a tapestry woven from the shared moments, support, and
inspiration gifted to me by the remarkable people in my life.

To my wife, Andrise: Your love is my greatest muse
and my steadfast anchor. You have been my partner in every
sense of the word, offering unwavering support and
boundless encouragement. Your belief in me, even in
moments when I doubted myself, has been the foundation
upon which this book was built. Thank you for being my
inspiration, my strength, and my greatest source of joy.

To my sister, Nanotte: You have been my rock, my
confidante, and my endless source of inspiration. Your
unwavering support and belief in me have been a constant
light, guiding me through every moment of doubt. Every
word I've written carries the love and encouragement you've
so selflessly given, and I am forever grateful for your
presence in my life.

To my friends: Thank you for your belief in my voice and your unshakable faith in my dreams. In moments of doubt, you lifted me up; in moments of triumph, you cheered the loudest. Your insights, honesty, and unwavering encouragement have made this journey richer, and I am profoundly thankful for your presence in my life.

To my readers and fans: Your passion for my poetry fills me with purpose and inspiration. Knowing my words have touched your hearts is the greatest reward of this odyssey. Your enthusiasm propels me to explore new realms of creativity and gives my work its truest meaning.

To every reader holding this book: Thank you for opening your heart to my words and allowing them to resonate within you. It is my deepest hope that these poems spark reflection, stir emotions, and inspire you in your own journey.

This book is a celebration of connection—the ties that bind us, the love that sustains us, and the resilience that propels us forward. Thank you for walking this poetic path with me. Your support is a gift, and I look forward to sharing many more adventures through words with you in the future.

With heartfelt gratitude,

About the Author

Samil is a visionary poet, celebrated author, and multifaceted artist whose work resonates across cultural and creative boundaries. With deep roots in Afro-Haitian heritage, Samil brings the richness of his cultural history to life through evocative poetry that champions resilience, love, and the boundless human spirit. His distinctive voice speaks to readers globally, offering profound insights that are both intensely personal and universally inspiring.

In *My Poetic Odyssey*, Samil delivers a masterful collection that explores themes of passion, identity, nature, culture, and transformation. Each poem is a doorway into a world of reflection and discovery, where the complexities of life are rendered in language both beautiful and profound. This collection is more than poetry—it's a journey that inspires readers to embrace their own paths with courage and hope.

Beyond the realm of poetry, Samil's artistic influence extends into music, where he has released two albums as a DJ. These works highlight his dynamic creativity and ability to tell stories through rhythm and sound. His literary journey began with the debut of *The Guardian of Morality*, a thought-provoking book that cemented his reputation as a storyteller of depth and substance.

When he isn't creating, Samil draws inspiration from life's quieter moments. Whether watching sports, delving into history and politics, or reflecting on the human condition, these interests fuel his work with a distinctive blend of insight and authenticity. His poetry embodies a timeless quality that bridges the past and present, making it relevant to readers of all generations.

Samil is passionate about using his art to spark meaningful dialogue and foster a deeper appreciation for the diversity that unites humanity. Through *My Poetic Odyssey* and his broader body of work, he invites readers to connect, celebrate shared experiences, and find strength in the beauty of their journeys.

For more about Samil and his work, visit
https://www.tiktok.com/@mypoeticodyssey
https://www.youtube.com/@mypoeticodyssey

THANK YOU